CONTENTS

FOREWORD

DARA Ó BRIAIN

We have an old saying in Ireland: "Ná lorg sneachta te, nuair atá báisteach tirim ar fáil." Translated from the Irish language it means: "Don't wish for warm snow when you can have dry rain."

I remember my grandfather saying this, as he shook his head slowly at whatever modern foolishness of ours he was watching unfold, and then he would stare out to sea, his gnarled farmer's hands twisted round his wooden walking stick as he carried with him the wisdom and suffering of generations of Irish people.

Don't wish for warm snow when you can have dry rain.

People would often say to me, "What does it mean, Dara, this ancient Irish saying, passed on to you by your wise grandfather as he sat amidst the fishing boats, tending to his nets, with the soil of the ground that he farmed his entire life under his fingernails?"

And I would say to them: "I do not know." I do not know what he meant, my weathered grandfather, who was both a fisherman and farmer, but also a gifted fiddle player, despite his hands being twisted by the years spent both fishing and farming, but also that time he fought for Ireland's independence, sometime when he wasn't busy fishing, farming and learning to play the violin to an acceptable standard.

Did I mention he rode horses as well? Tamed them and learned their ways and I suppose, taught them his ways, this increasingly unlikely grandfather of mine, when he wasn't previously engaged in fishing, farming, fiddling and fighting for Ireland's independence, which must have taken up much of his time.

I do not know what he meant, when he said that old Irish saying that I previously claimed that he would often say, amidst his busy schedule of fish, horses, milking, violin-playing and revolutionary uprisings, because, as I think is probably becoming clear, I made both him and the saying up.

IRELAND

The people

The places

The stories

Rachel Pierce with a foreword by **Dara Ó Briain**

■ SCHOLASTIC

FOR DONAGH, ERRIS, MEEDA AND CONNE

A note on the maps in this book

The maps in this book are for illustrative purposes only and should not be relied on for accuracy. For a comprehensive and accurate map of Ireland, please visit maps.ie.

A note on the pronunciation of Irish words

Every effort has been made to ensure that this information is correct at the time of going to print. Any errors will be corrected upon reprint. For a comprehensive dictionary and language library, please visit teanglann.ie.

Published in the UK by Scholastic, 2021
Euston House, 24 Eversholt Street, London, NW1 1DB
Scholastic Ireland, 89E Lagan Road, Dublin Industrial Estate, Glasnevin, Dublin, D11 HP5F

SCHOLASTIC and associated logos are trademarks and/or registered trademarks of Scholastic Inc.

Text © Rachel Pierce, 2021
Foreword © Dara Ó Briain, 2021

Illustration for 'The Island of Ireland' © Linda Fahrlin, 2021
Illustration for 'Early Ireland' © Diarmuid Ó Catháin, 2021
Illustration for 'Warring Ireland' © Alan Dunne, 2021
Illustration for 'Haunted Ireland' © Lydia Hughes, 2021
Illustration for 'Magical Ireland' © Brian Fitzgerald, 2021
Illustration for 'The Living Landscape' © Ashling Lindsay, 2021
Illustration for 'The Human Landscape' © Graham Corcoran, 2021
Illustration for 'Underground Ireland' © Jennifer Farley, 2021
Illustration for 'The Culture of Ireland' © Conor Nolan, 2021
Illustration for 'Fun Things to Do in Ireland' © Donough O'Malley, 2021

Cover illustration by Conor Nolan

Design by Plum 5 Ltd

ISBN 978 07023 0241 1

A CIP catalogue record for this book is available from the British Library.

Printed in China
Paper made from wood grown in sustainable forests and other controlled sources.

1 3 5 7 9 10 8 6 4 2

www.scholastic.co.uk

FSC
www.fsc.org

MIX
Paper from
responsible sources
FSC® C008047

In reality, I never met either of my grandfathers, although I did meet one grandmother and she did fight in the Irish War of Independence and that is a whole other story that we don't have time for here; she, like the rest of the family though, never had anything to do with fishing, horses or playing the violin.

And I can speak the Irish language fluently, so that translation is accurate, but I settled on that saying because I liked the rhythm of it.

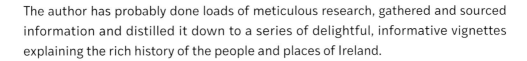

Welcome to a book about Ireland. I hope you like stories.

I mean, there might be facts in here too.

The author has probably done loads of meticulous research, gathered and sourced information and distilled it down to a series of delightful, informative vignettes explaining the rich history of the people and places of Ireland.

I presume so; I haven't read the book; I was too busy inventing fake sayings that my fake grandfather would have said if he had been real. I'm Irish; that's sort of what we do.

I'm not saying that it's an Irish trait to be inaccurate or dishonest; we have many great scientists and doctors and writers and other jobs where truth is important. We just happen to also have lots of storytellers; and while checking facts and getting things right are really, really admirable skills and we totally recommend doing that, we also quite enjoy just telling a good yarn alongside, or indeed, instead of, the truth.

Take the case of Aileen's Wave.

Aileen's Wave is a huge swell of water off the County Clare coast. Beloved by surfers and assorted daredevils, this particular wave arrives as a result of swells in the Atlantic Ocean, drawn by the tidal pull of the Moon, sped across the shallowing of the underwater shelf, until it crashes, abruptly, against the Clare shore, its energy suddenly dispersed across the Cliffs of Moher.

It should be enough that it's a really big wave. Big waves are fun and loud and dramatic. It should be sufficiently exciting that it's a big wave smashing against a huge cliff. Imagine that sight, the coast battered by the great Atlantic Ocean (working in tandem with the Moon, no less!) that you can watch from the cliff-top while thrill-seekers on wooden boards try to stay alive far below you. That should be enough.

But NO! This is Ireland. We have to stick a story on top of all this.

Apparently ... the wave ... is haunted.

Oh, did you not hear me? Maybe you should lean in closer. Lean in, while the firelight flickers, and the shadows gather around us; I'll tell you the story of St Patrick and the ancient gods and seven horses in a cave.

I'm not kidding, you can read all about it on page 57.

It couldn't just be a wave. It had to be a haunted wave, made by ghost horses. We couldn't just enjoy the big splash without sticking a story on top of it.

So why do we keep making up all these stories? Why do we attach myth and legend to every upturned stone and withered tree in the country? Here's a clue.

Turn to the index of this book and look for all the mentions of 'active volcanoes' in Ireland.

I'll give you a minute and then come back here.

What? You didn't find any? Okay, then look up hurricanes.

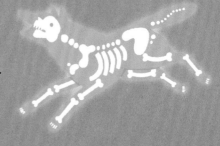

No? Whirlpools? Deserts? Jungles?
Snow-capped mountains?

Nothing like that? Hmmm. Is there anything interesting happening in this landscape at all?

Okay then, let's try something else. Go back to the index and try to find all the mentions of tigers in Ireland.

No? How about elephants? Bears?

Not a mention of ANY of them? Did you look up great apes? Killer whales? Unicorns? Is there even a decent-sized spider anywhere on this island? Is there anything that you couldn't fend off with a shoe?

Some people don't need stories because where they live, wild and crazy things are happening all the time. "Our village was attacked by a python," they will say. "Really?" say Irish people, "because I think I stepped in some nettles recently. I mean, I was wearing trousers so it wouldn't have hurt anyway, but still, you have to be careful."

Ireland is a small, safe island. People don't get whooshed up by geysers, devoured by hippos, carried off by eagles, sucked into quicksand, skeletonized by piranha, chased by lava or frozen into glaciers. You can't even get lost in Ireland because we all know each other, and somebody will find you and bring you home.

But the nights are long, and it rains a lot, so we have lots of time indoors; we learned how to make up stories instead.

So, approach this book with an open mind. And a pinch of salt. Everything here might be true; but also, as my grandfather used to say, "If the story is good, does it matter if it's true or not?" And with that, he would wink at me, throw his violin over his shoulder and ride his horse into the sea.

INTRODUCTION

WHAT DO YOU KNOW?

Here's a quick quiz to see how well you know Ireland.

WHAT IS THE NATIONAL COLOUR OF IRELAND?

You are probably familiar with the flag of Ireland. It's a tricolour: green, white and orange. It has been used as Ireland's flag since 1916. It's important to put the colours in the correct order or it looks like the flag of the Ivory Coast!

Why is it green, white and orange? The colours have meanings.
Green represents the Roman Catholic faith.
Orange represents the Protestant faith.
White is a symbol of peace between both faiths.

But did you know that these are not the national colours of Ireland? It's sometimes called the Emerald Isle, so lots of people think that the national colour of Ireland is green. It's not. The traditional national colour of Ireland is St Patrick's blue.

ARE THERE WALLABIES IN IRELAND?

Wallabies are found in Australia, of course!
Really? No!

There *are* wallabies in Ireland. Crazy as it sounds, a colony of about one hundred red-necked wallabies lives on Lambay Island, 4 kilometres (2.5 miles) off the coast of North County Dublin. The family that owns the island introduced the wallabies there and now they are thriving. They are a long way from the hot weather of Australia, but they have adapted to the rain. It's even been said that they speak 'a few words' (*cúpla focail*, coop-la fuk-el) of Irish when no one's listening!

Now you know something about Ireland that lots of people don't know! Time to find out more...

THE ISLAND OF IRELAND

Canada 5,767km / 3,583 miles
Greenland 2,624km / 1,630 miles

IRELAND

Population: 5.5 million

N

NW   NE

W   E

SW   SE

S

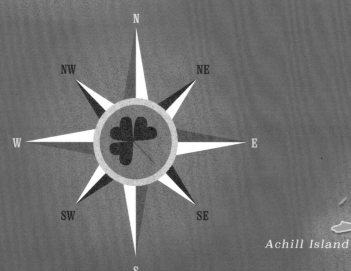

Sligo

Achill Island

Mayo

Ros-
common

Omey Island

Atlantic Ocean

Galway

Connacht

Aran Islands

Clare

Tippe-
rary

Limerick

Munster

MOST
WESTERLY
POINT

Kerry

LARGEST COUNTY

Tearaght Island
is the last stop
before America!

Tearaght Island

Great Blasket
Island

Cork

Cork city is the
capital of Munster.

Old Head

The wreck
of RMS
Lusitania
lies on the
seabed here.

USA 6,650km / 4,132 miles

MOST
SOUTHERLY
POINT

Fastnet

MOST NORTHERLY POINT

Inishtrahull

Iceland 1,422km / 883 miles

Giant's Causeway

There are thirty-two counties on the island of Ireland. Six of them are part of the United Kingdom: counties Antrim, Armagh, Down, Fermanagh, Derry and Tyrone. Together they are called Northern Ireland. The capital city is Belfast. This line shows the point where the Republic of Ireland meets Northern Ireland.

Donegal

Derry

Antrim

Tyrone

Ulster

Lough Neagh

Down

Cannon Rock

Fermanagh

Armagh

MOST EASTERLY POINT

Monaghan

Smallest County The "wee county"

Scotland 23km / 14 miles

Leitrim

Cavan

Louth

Longford

Westmeath

Meath

In 1774, Sir Francis Beaufort was born in Navan, County Meath. He was an admiral in the British navy. He wanted to make life at sea safer for sailors, so he invented the Beaufort scale. It categorizes wind speeds from Force 1 to Force 12 and it's still in use today.

Leinster

Kildare

Dublin

Kish

Offaly

Laois

Wicklow

Dublin is the capital city of Ireland.

Carlow

Kilkenny

Irish Sea

Wexford

1172

Waterford

Hook Head

England 490km / 304 miles

Hook Head is the oldest working lighthouse in the world.

St George's Channel

Spain 1,485km / 922 miles

Wales 128 miles / 79 miles

THE ISLAND OF IRELAND

That Ireland is an island is hugely important for its history and its people. Ireland is the third largest island in Europe and lies at the edge of the Eurasian land mass. An island can be a safe place to be because it's difficult to reach. Or it can be a dangerous place to be, all alone and tempting to invaders. Ireland has been a safe haven and at risk throughout its often violent and bloody history.

The island of Ireland is quite small – it would take about 115 islands of Ireland to make up the size of the United States – but it contains very varied landscapes and is extremely beautiful. If you arrive by sea to the east coast, you will find a ragged coastline, with lots of nooks and crannies where smugglers could hide and invaders could sneak in. It's important to sail carefully around these waters because there are many rocks and sandbanks lurking beneath the waves. This is proved by the huge number of shipwrecks that lie abandoned on the seabed all around Ireland's coast. There is a whole underwater history down there.

Once you come safely ashore, you meet a very green land of rolling fields, wide rivers and high mountains. But the landscape can change suddenly. You might be travelling across the grassy sloping fields of County Clare, then suddenly find yourself in the strange, rocky world that is known as the Burren. It's a limestone karst region where the rocky terrain looks as if it has been melted into smooth, curving shapes.

If you travel north and north-east, you find the towering black cliffs of the North Antrim coast and Donegal, pounded by the white-topped waves of the Atlantic Ocean. If you travel west, you meet the bright yellow furze, purple heathers and stone walls of Connemara.

If you travel south, you enjoy the lush warmth of the south-east and the breathtaking mountain passes of Cork and Kerry.

Ireland is an island of sudden surprises.

Brent geese

Spotted flycatcher

Swallow

House martin

Sand martin

Cuckoo

Willow warbler

The **spring migration** brings visiting birds to Ireland and sees others, who have overwintered here, taking their leave and heading to distant countries. Around 140 different species visit the west coast each year, including Canada geese, swallows and cuckoos. The amazing thing is that these birds often cover thousands of miles as they seek out warmer weather or food sources. They are hardy and intrepid travellers – and a very welcome sight when they arrive, bringing the spring with them.

GEOLOGY

The story of Ireland is told by its rocks – that's about 1.7 billion years of natural history under our feet. The oldest are Precambrian, found in Mayo and Donegal in the north-west. Around 500 million years ago there was no island of Ireland. It was in two parts, separated by the Iapetus Ocean. About 400 million years ago, the south-eastern and north-western halves collided, forming mountain ranges where they met. It's hard to imagine now, but 350 million years ago Ireland was covered by a tropical sea and 240 million years ago the island had a desert climate. Over the last 300,000 years, the Ireland we know today was formed, mainly from massive glaciers scraping, bumping and melting their way across the country. When you're out walking on the beaches or in the mountains, remember to keep an eye out for fossils embedded in stones. You could end up holding a few million years of history in your hand!

LIGHTHOUSES

The coast of Ireland is watched over by seventy lighthouses. Since 1997, they are all operated automatically, so there are no lighthouse-keepers living in them. But for the rest of their history, stretching back hundreds of years, there was always at least one keeper living on site and tending the light. This was tough work and often lonely, but it was crucial because it saved lives. Hook Head is the oldest lighthouse, but Fastnet is the tallest and widest. It stands on barren Fastnet Rock, off the coast of Cork, and is 54 metres (177 feet) high and built of thick granite to withstand the battering waves. The strangest lighthouse must be the Spire of Lloyd in Kells, County Meath. It looks like a lighthouse and is tall and sturdy with a glazed lantern, but it's nowhere near the sea. In fact, it's a mock lighthouse, built by the first Earl of Bective in 1791 to honour his father. It gives views across five counties – but no waves or seagulls!

ISLANDS

Ireland is said to have about eighty main offshore islands, although there are hundreds of islets and rocky crags, so it's hard to count properly. The largest is Achill Island, off the coast of County Mayo, which is connected to the mainland by a road bridge that crosses Achill Sound. The island may win the

Aran Islands

Tearaght Island

title of largest, but it's still only about 24 km (15 miles) across. Omey Island, off County Galway, is also connected to the mainland – but only at low tide. When the tide goes out, it uncovers a causeway of sand that you can cross to reach the island. But you have to be very careful. When the tide races back, Omey becomes an island again and you're stuck there until the next low tide – although it's a pretty incredible place to be stuck!

On Inishmore, one of the Aran Islands, the massive Dún Aonghasa prehistoric hilltop fort squats on the edge of a high cliff. Long ago, islands were often home to monks who wanted a life of silence. That tradition hasn't died out completely. Some of the islands have just three or four people living on them. Great Blasket Island invites two people to live alone on the island from April to October to act as caretakers. Now that's a quiet life!

SMUGGLERS, PIRATES & SHIPWRECKS

Islands have often been interesting places for smugglers. They may steal valuable things from the island and smuggle them to another country, or they may smuggle goods on to the island – wine, brandy and luxury items that can be sold for good money. It's a dangerous job, though. There are cold and dangerous seas and guards to dodge. Many places around the coast are famed for smuggling, such as Dalkey in Dublin. Wine and brandy from Spain and France were floated into a cave in the dead of night and then spirited away along deserted roads. That's how Smuggler's Cave in Dalkey got its name.

By far the strangest and saddest tale of smuggling in Ireland, though, is known as the Sack of Baltimore. One night in June 1631, a band of Barbary pirates crept into the seaside village of Baltimore and stole away virtually the entire village – men, women and children – into slavery in Algiers, in north Africa, about 3,000 km (1,900 miles) away from Cork. It was a daring and despicable act.

Of all the many shipwrecks on the seabed around Ireland's coast, the most famous is RMS *Lusitania*. It was a huge passenger liner that was travelling from New York to Liverpool when it was hit by a torpedo from a German submarine on 7 May 1915. One of the passengers was Hugh Lane, an art collector and founder of the Hugh Lane Gallery in Dublin. It is said that he was accompanied by priceless artworks by Rembrandt and Monet. We will never know because the ship sank and everything aboard was lost, along with 1,198 lives. The wreck lies about 18 km (11 miles) from the Old Head of Kinsale lighthouse.

500 MILLION YEARS AGO
Ireland is in two parts, separated by an ocean

65 MILLION YEARS AGO
The basalt 'stepping stones' of the Giant's Causeway in County Antrim are formed

300 MILLION YEARS AGO
The limestone of the Burren is laid down

MESOLITHIC PERIOD
8000–4000 BC

1.7 BILLION YEARS AGO
Ireland's oldest rocks are laid down

240 MILLION YEARS AGO
Ireland has a desert climate

400 MILLION YEARS AGO
The two parts collide and join

8000–7000 BC
The first settlers arrive in Ireland

WOULD YOU BELIEVE IT?

Amelia Earhart landed in a field in County Derry on her west-to-east Atlantic solo flight in 1929, the first woman to fly this route solo. It took about 15 hours to fly from Newfoundland, on the east coast of North America, to Northern Ireland. Her intended destination was Paris, but bad weather and some technical issues with her aeroplane forced a change of plan. Down she came in a green field, surprising the locals. She was a brave pilot, but her adventures ended mysteriously when her plane vanished in July 1937 while she was flying across the Pacific Ocean. No trace of the plane or Amelia has ever been found. There is a museum in Derry to commemorate her historic landing there.

Achill Island

Dooagh Beach on Achill Island disappeared in the winter of 1984 and for over thirty years it was just a memory for local people. Imagine their surprise when they woke up one morning in April 2017 and the beach was there again! The locals enjoyed walking its sandy stretch, delighted that the sea had given it back to them. Fast forward to January 2019, when overnight they found that every single grain of sand had gone. The beach had performed its disappearing trick again.

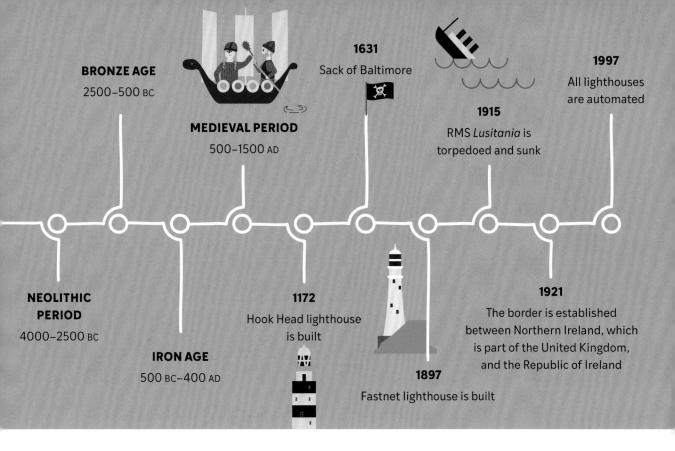

BRONZE AGE
2500–500 BC

MEDIEVAL PERIOD
500–1500 AD

1631
Sack of Baltimore

1915
RMS *Lusitania* is
torpedoed and sunk

1997
All lighthouses
are automated

**NEOLITHIC
PERIOD**
4000–2500 BC

1172
Hook Head lighthouse
is built

1921
The border is established
between Northern Ireland, which
is part of the United Kingdom,
and the Republic of Ireland

IRON AGE
500 BC–400 AD

1897
Fastnet lighthouse is built

Lough Neagh is the largest lake in Ireland and Britain. It covers an area of 396 square km (153 sq. miles). It is famed for its beauty as much as its great size.

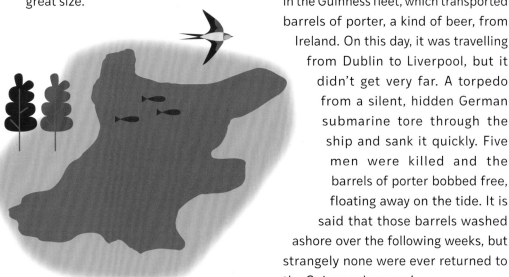

The Kish lighthouse has seen a lot of wrecks in its waters, including that of the steamship **W.M. Barkley** on 12 October 1917. This was the first ship in the Guinness fleet, which transported barrels of porter, a kind of beer, from Ireland. On this day, it was travelling from Dublin to Liverpool, but it didn't get very far. A torpedo from a silent, hidden German submarine tore through the ship and sank it quickly. Five men were killed and the barrels of porter bobbed free, floating away on the tide. It is said that those barrels washed ashore over the following weeks, but strangely none were ever returned to the Guinness brewery!

EARLY IRELAND

THE CÉIDE FIELDS,
COUNTY MAYO

CREEVYKEEL
COURT TOMB
COUNTY SLIG

RATHCROGHAN. COUNTY ROSCOMMON

POULNABRONE DOLMEN. THE BURREN

DÚN AONGHASA,
COUNTY GALWAY

DROMBEG STONE
CIRCLE. COUNTY CORK

THE GRIANAN OF AILEACH, COUNTY DONEGAL, SAID TO BE THE SLEEPING PLACE OF ANCIENT AND FEARSOME GIANTS

MOUNT SANDEL, COUNTY DERRY

EMLAGH BOG, COUNTY MEATH

THE BOA ISLAND FIGURE, COUNTY FERMANAGH

NAVAN FORT, COUNTY ARMAGH

CLONYCAVAN MAN FOUND NEAR HERE

OLD CROGHAN MAN FOUND NEAR HERE

THE UNESCO WORLD HERITAGE SITE AT NEWGRANGE

FOURKNOCKS MEGALITHIC PASSAGE TOMB, COUNTY MEATH

THE 30-M (100-FT) HIGH ROUND TOWER OF GLENDALOUGH, COUNTY WICKLOW, THE SITE OF ST KEVIN'S MONASTERY

THE ROCK OF CASHEL, COUNTY TIPPERARY

THE HILL OF TARA, COUNTY MEATH

THE VIKINGS ARRIVED IN AD 795, LANDING FIRST AT LAMBAY ISLAND, COUNTY DUBLIN

EARLY IRELAND

The human history of Ireland is quite a bit shorter than its geological history. It is about 12,000 years, as far as we know. The earliest humans on the island had to contend with ice sheets and brown bears on the prowl, so it wasn't an easy existence. The first really impressive signs of past humans seem to date from the Neolithic period, about 3,000 years ago, when the cycle of life and death was honoured by the building of magnificent tombs, like the famous site at Newgrange in County Meath.

Until 2016, it was accepted that the first humans to live in Ireland arrived around 8,000 BC, coming across the sea 10,000 years ago to explore a speck of land on the horizon and then making it their home. But that story was thrown into doubt when archaeologists found a bear bone with cut marks on it.

The funny thing was that they found the bone in a box in the National Museum in Dublin, not under the ground as you might expect. It had been sitting in the box since the 1920s, having been found in 1903 in Alice and Gwendoline Cave in County Clare. The cave was named after two ladies who lived in a nearby manor house. When the bone was rediscovered and examined in 2016, the marks turned out to be butchery marks on fresh bone, which could only have been made by a human using a flint blade of some kind.

The story of humans in Ireland now begins about 12,000 years ago, when that bear had its flesh hacked from its bones. It means that Palaeolithic or Old Stone Age people were living on the island then, which no one had proved before. That's why archaeology is such an exciting job – one find can change the history of a whole country!

HUNTING AND GATHERING

In the Mesolithic era, around 8000 BC, the hunter–gatherers foraged and made weapons to hunt birds and animals. The main site where we can learn about the Mesolithic people is at Mount Sandel in County Derry, where a band of people made their home on the banks of the River Bann. They built simple houses with wooden frames covered in hides – the first houses built in Ireland, as far as we know. There were probably only a few thousand people living on the whole island then and it's likely they largely stayed around the coastal areas.

THE CÉIDE FIELDS

By about 4000 BC, people living on the island of Ireland had begun farming. Learning how to grow and harvest their own food meant they could set up home in one spot and stay there because they were able to work the land. The Céide Fields in Mayo show the remains of stone walls, houses and tombs, all preserved in the bog land. The Céide Fields are thought to be the oldest field systems in the world.

THE MATHEMATICS OF WORSHIP

The Neolithic period (which began around 3500 BC) was an incredible time in Irish history. Once people had shelter and food, they could turn their thoughts to other things – such as contemplating the sky, the sun and the stars, and what happened to their loved ones when they died. These may have been the imaginings of the tomb-builders who left hundreds of tombs of different types all over the country. Newgrange is the most famous of all – and it's older than the Great Pyramids of Egypt. Satellite tombs, some smaller and some large, like Knowth and Dowth, surround the main tomb. The whole complex is known as Brú na Bóinne, 'the palace of the Boyne'. But these aren't just burial places for the dead. They are also feats of mathematics because the tombs are aligned with the path of the sun. Newgrange itself is aligned with the rising sun at the winter solstice (21 December), which is the shortest day of the year. If clouds don't ruin it, on the morning of the solstice the sun's rays slowly penetrate the deep darkness of the tomb through a roof-box above the entrance. A shaft of sunlight stretches into the cold, silent tomb. It's an unforgettable sight.

THE ROYAL SITE AT TARA

There were six important royal sites in ancient Ireland, and the Hill of Tara was considered one of the most sacred. It was the inauguration site of the high kings of Tara, where the ritual ceremony of making a new king was performed. There are burials in the many mounds on the hill and cremated remains, pots, necklaces and a dagger have been found there. Standing on top of the Forradh (for-ahh; royal seat) is the Lia Fáil (lee-ah foil) – the stone of destiny.

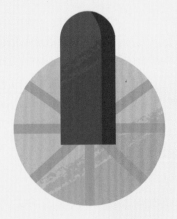

This is a magical stone. It was said that when a worthy king was chosen, the stone roared out its approval.

DEFENDED FORTS

The huge stone hill forts were mainly built in the Iron Age, when people had discovered how to make tools and weapons from iron. There was always a chance of a marauding band turning up, so hill forts were designed as places of safety and defence. There were some ingenious ideas to keep out would-be invaders. At Dún Aonghasa, on Inishmore, County Galway, the massive dry-stone hill fort was surrounded by a chevaux-de-frise. This was an army of small stone slabs, planted upright in the ground. They prevented horses being

able to race at the fort and also forced visitors to pick their way carefully, which slowed them down. It was the Iron Age version of a burglar alarm.

BOG BODIES

The skin looks like ancient leather – blackened, shrivelled and puckered. The yellowed teeth are still there, jutting out of the jawbones. The fingernails are there, though they are black and sunken. The hair still covers the squashed skull. The features of the face are sunken but can still be made out. The body has collapsed and flattened. And there are wounds that speak of a violent death.

This is Clonycavan man, a bog body unearthed in County Meath in 2003. About 120 bog bodies have been found in Ireland. Two of the best preserved are Clonycavan man and Old Croghan man, now on display in the National Museum, Dublin. The reason they are

so well preserved is that peat bogs are low in oxygen and high in acid, so they mummify the body and prevent decomposition. The bog bodies are strange to look at and a bit of a mystery. Clonycavan man had received several blows to the head with a sharp tool like an axe. Old Croghan man – who stood about 2 m (6 ft 6 in) tall – had holes cut in his arms for a rope of hazel to be passed through. The bogs were seen as a place between worlds – neither on Earth nor in the afterlife – and this may be why these young men were killed and buried there. Were they the victims of ritual killings? Was the bog burial a punishment of some kind? We might never know.

c. 8000 BC
Hunter–gatherers of the Mesolithic era are active

c. 3500 BC
Neolithic people honour their dead by placing their cremated remains in stone tombs

c. 500 BC – c. AD 400
The Iron Age is the time of massive hill forts and ring forts, of royal sites and kingship, and of the Celts

c. 10,000 BC
Early people butcher a brown bear in a cave in County Clare

4000 BC
The start of farming and field systems

c. 1800 BC
Bronze Age people make beautiful bronze and gold jewellery

362–175 BC
Sometime between these dates, Old Croghan man is brutally murdered and buried in a bog in County Offaly

WOULD YOU BELIEVE IT?

Ogham writing is the earliest writing in Irish that we know of. No paper or pen was involved – the writer scored lines on a tall, upright stone. Those lines represented letters of the alphabet. It was mainly used to commemorate a person's name. The majority of these stones are found in the south of the country, in Kerry, Cork and Waterford.

Fourknocks is a 5,000-year-old passage tomb in County Meath. There is a black iron door set into the tomb entrance and your visit starts by making a trip down the road to the house of the keyholder. You borrow the key, unlock the door and step inside the ancient darkness of the cold tomb. A passage opens out into a large chamber, and as your eyes get used to the dim light, you can make out some beautiful rock art. The remains of sixty-five burials – adults and children – have been found there, along with grave goods.

The *cailleach* (kai-lock) was an old hag or witch with supernatural powers. She is linked with many sites and the clue is usually in the name. So, Loughcrew in Irish is *Slieve na Calliagh* (sh-leave na kai-lock) – 'the cailleach's mountain'. Loughcrew is a passage-tomb cemetery on a hilltop in County Meath. Legend says that the hills around Loughcrew were formed when a giant cailleach went striding across the country and dropped rocks from her apron.

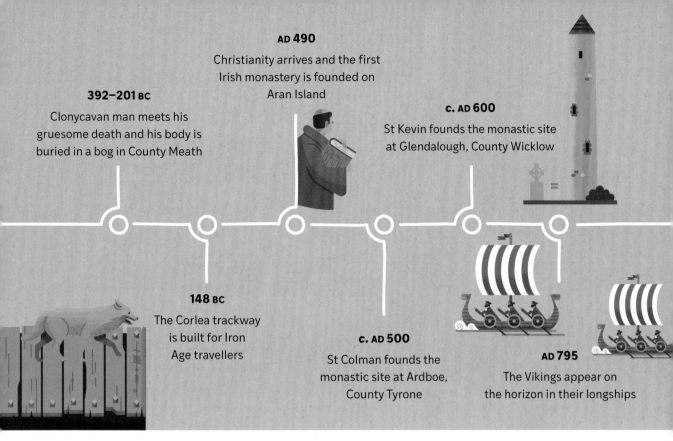

392–201 BC
Clonycavan man meets his gruesome death and his body is buried in a bog in County Meath

AD 490
Christianity arrives and the first Irish monastery is founded on Aran Island

c. AD 600
St Kevin founds the monastic site at Glendalough, County Wicklow

148 BC
The Corlea trackway is built for Iron Age travellers

c. AD 500
St Colman founds the monastic site at Ardboe, County Tyrone

AD 795
The Vikings appear on the horizon in their longships

The bogs of Ireland have preserved many bodies, but they were also used to preserve something else. Butter! In 2009, a 35-kilogram (77-pound) lump of butter in an oak barrel was found in a bog in County Kildare. And in 2016, a 10kg (22lb) lump was found in Emlagh bog in County Meath that was 2,000 years old. The size of these lumps suggest they might have been a community's butter store. Even though they are so old, the bog has done its job and they still smell of butter and are said to be edible.

Round towers were freestanding bell towers, but it is likely they were also used to store valuable objects. A monastery's most precious items, such as chalices and illuminated manuscripts, could be stashed away at the top of the round tower in the hope that marauding Vikings couldn't reach them.

The Celts were the people who lived in Iron Age Europe. We have been able to learn about their beliefs thanks to the art and monuments they left behind. They also left epic poems and tales that describe their view of gods and goddesses. The Celts believed that everything had its own spirit – from stones and trees to rivers and mountains. So, for example, Boann was the goddess of the River Boyne. These beliefs were more than just blood-stirring tales of powerful beings – they were part of the whole way of life of the Celts. And part of their way of death, as the ancient tombs show us.

WARRING IRELAND

GRANUAILE'S CASTLE,
CLARE ISLAND

DOONAGORE
CASTLE

PALLAS CASTLE

BUNRATTY CASTLE

TULLAUN
CASTLE

KING JOHN'S CASTLE, LIMERICK

BLARNEY CASTLE

DUNLUCE CASTLE

CARRICKFERGUS CASTLE

CLOUGH CASTLE

KING JOHN'S CASTLE,
CARLINGFORD

CASTLE ROCHE

TRIM CASTLE

ARDGILLAN CASTLE

BIRR CASTLE

LEAP CASTLE

DUBLIN CASTLE

ROCK OF
DUNAMASE

RUSSBOROUGH
HOUSE

KILKENNY CASTLE

WARRING IRELAND

The bloody history of Ireland became even bloodier in the Middle Ages. The poor people got poorer. The rich got richer. If you had wealth and power, you also had a lot to lose. As a result, those with money began to build castles and fortified homes to protect themselves. The Normans arrived on Irish shores in 1169 and brought with them the idea of the Norman castle, motte-and-bailey and tower house. These were sturdy buildings with cruel and ingenious systems for defending and attacking. Medieval Ireland wasn't for the faint-hearted!

We are entering a time of wall-building, when Irish people constructed defences to keep out unwanted visitors. They built walls around their homes and castles and even bigger and longer walls around their towns. There were twenty-nine walled towns in Ireland. Of course, when you build a wall, you build a target. An invader sees a wall and immediately wants to know what's hidden behind it. If they can't march straight in, there's always the option of sitting outside until everyone inside starves to death, or maybe shooting a few fiery arrows over the walls so the citizens come staggering out, clutching their smoke-filled throats in surrender.

The arrival of the Anglo-Normans on Irish shores was the start of a long, long battle over Ireland. The country's neighbour, England, wanted to take Ireland into its growing realm. The Irish weren't exactly delighted with this proposition. Both sides fought to gain the upper hand, and the fighting lasted for hundreds of years. It made Ireland a very dangerous place to live, which is why all the walls were needed. This was a particularly bloody period in Irish history.

CASTLE FEATURES

Irish castles had some very interesting features. A trip step was a stairwell designed to trip up an attacker. The steps were different heights or uneven, and the stairwell curved around as it ascended. The attacker coming up the stairs would have his sword hand against the wall, making it awkward to swing his sword arm effectively. The advantage was with the defender, coming down the other way.

Castles had narrow, rectangular windows through which an arrow could be shot, but an archer outside could never shoot an arrow in through them. Some castles also had murder holes. These were holes in the ceiling, usually in the lobby, through which rocks or arrows could be thrown down on to attackers. There are plenty of examples of murder holes, including

at Tullaun Castle in County Tipperary, Carrickfergus Castle in County Antrim and Blarney Castle in County Cork.

There is a popular idea that defenders poured boiling oil down on the heads of their tormentors. That would have been highly effective, but it's unlikely. They would have used things that were easily available and that didn't pose so much of a danger to themselves. A truly chilling feature of some castles was an oubliette, a 'forgotten place'. This was a dungeon room that had one way in and no way out. The way in was a hole in the dungeon roof, through which the enemy was flung. Bunratty Castle has one, and the oubliette at Leap Castle was the stuff of nightmares: it had wooden spikes sticking up out of the ground. When it was discovered, there were piles of human bones down there.

WELCOMING THE INVADERS

The arrival of the Anglo-Normans in Ireland changed the course of Irish history. One man's name is always mentioned when the Norman invasion is talked about: Diarmait Mac Murchada, or Dermot MacMurrough. In an attempt to regain the kingship of Leinster, which he lost after kidnapping the wife of the king of Breifne, Diarmait sought help from King Henry II of England. That led to the recruitment of an army of Norman-Welsh mercenaries, who arrived on Irish shores in 1169, led by Richard de Clare, second Earl of Pembroke, known as 'Strongbow'. Diarmait gave his daughter, Aoife, in marriage to Strongbow, with the promise that the groom would succeed to the kingship after his father-in-law. As so often happens in history, Diarmait couldn't control what happened next. The Normans spread out through Ireland, conquering and taking land as their own. Diarmait's short-sighted grab for power had long-lasting consequences. He was ever after known as 'Dermot of the foreigners'.

THE CASTLE ON THE CLIFF-EDGE

When you approach Dunluce Castle in Armagh from the east, the road bends around a corner and suddenly you see it: a great hulking ruin, black against the sky, perched at the edge of a sheer cliff. The castle has been standing on that wind-lashed cliff since 1500, when the McQuillans of Scotland built it. They lost it to the MacDonnells in 1554, and its most famous owner was probably Sorley Boy MacDonnell. It was he who plundered the remains of a wrecked Spanish Armada ship at the nearby Giant's Causeway and brought its cannons to Dunluce to become part of his defences.

About 25 m (82 ft) below the castle is the huge rocky cavern called Mermaid's Cave. It has a sad story: Maeve Roe, daughter of Lord McQuillan, refused to marry the man chosen by her father and was imprisoned in the tower. One night, she stole away with the man she did love, Reginald O'Cahan. They tried to escape in a rowing boat, but the waves picked it up and flung it against the bare cliffs – they both drowned. They say the sound of Maeve's weeping can still be heard on the wind.

TRIM CASTLE, COUNTY MEATH

The largest Anglo-Norman castle in Ireland is King John's Castle in Trim, County Meath. It's a massive three-storey keep surrounded by a great hall, stables, lime kilns and a sturdy gatehouse. Construction was started in 1176 by Hugh de Lacy and finished thirty years later by his son. The castle was designed to be almost impossible to besiege or overrun.

When you entered the castle, your nose might twitch at a nasty, wafting smell. That would be the garderobe, where clothes were hung up over the open toilet. Strange as it sounds, the fumes from the household's poo killed any lice and fleas crawling on the clothes.

FAMOUS BATTLES

At the Battle of Clontarf in 1014, the massed troops of Brian Boru took on a bloodthirsty Viking army. The men fought all day at close quarters with swords. In the end Boru won and it marked the end of the Vikings' push to take over the island.

Battles by the Boyne in County Meath (1690) and at Aughrim in County Galway (1691) pitched Jacobites (loyal to King James II) against Williamites (loyal to King William III). The fight was for the crown and to maintain the Protestant religion in Ireland. At the battle site in 1690, 25,000 Jacobites faced 36,000 Williamites across the River Boyne, fighting with musket guns and cannons. The battle ended with the Jacobites beating a hasty retreat. A year later, they faced each other again at Aughrim. It turned out to be one of the bloodiest battles ever fought on Irish soil, with about 7,000 bodies littering the

field when it ended. James II's claim to the crown died that day as well. His army's loss was decisive and William kept the throne.

One hundred years later, battles were still being fought between the Catholic Irish and the Protestant English. Thousands of British troops surrounded County Wexford in 1798, determined to crush the rebellion of the United Irishmen. The rebel forces stood firm and the battle raged at Vinegar Hill. The British forces were well equipped with musket guns, field guns, cannon and shrapnel shells. The rebels were eventually forced to retreat, but it's what happened after the battle that was truly shocking. In 2017, archaeologists found large pits at the site, containing the remains of about 2,000 women, children and elderly people. They were killed to send a message to rebels everywhere: if you persist, you will suffer.

1014
Battle of Clontarf

1169
The Anglo-Normans land in
Ireland at Bannow Bay

1170
Strongbow marries Aoife

1200s
Norman buildings – castles and
town walls – spring up everywhere

c. 1202
Trim Castle is completed

c. 1210
Kilkenny Castle
is completed

c. 1210
King John's Castle in Limerick
is completed

1230
Dublin Castle
is completed

c. 1250
The first Bunratty
Castle is built

1446
Blarney Castle is completed

c. 1500
Dunluce Castle is completed

c. 1550
Doonagore Castle is built

1500s
Granuaile's Castle on
Clare Island is built

1588
Spanish Armada ships are wrecked
on Ireland's Atlantic coast

1601–02
Siege of Kinsale

1620
Birr Castle is built

1649
Siege of Drogheda

1689
Siege of Derry

1690
Battle of the Boyne

1691
Battle of Aughrim

1798
Battle of Vinegar Hill

WOULD YOU BELIEVE IT?

Derry is the only walled town in Ireland with all its walls intact. About 1.6 km (1 mile) of walls encircle the town. They are 105 m (35 ft) thick in places.

Birr Castle, in County Offaly, could once boast of having the largest telescope on Earth! It was built in the grounds of the castle by keen astronomer the third Earl of Rosse, completed in 1845, and had a 183 cm (72-inch) reflector. It was called the Leviathan. It remained the biggest telescope until 1917.

Blarney Castle in County Cork was built by the McCarthy family as a stronghold. It's famous for the Stone of Eloquence. Better known as the Blarney Stone, it is the reason that visitors hang upside down over a sheer drop. The legend is that if you lean backwards and kiss the stone, you will be rewarded with eloquence – you'll never be lost for words again. While strolling in the grounds, be careful not to get too close to the plants in the Poison Garden. The poisonous plants growing there include wolfsbane, mandrake and ricin. The sign says not to touch, smell or eat them – you've been warned!

The **Rock of Dunamase** in County Laois was a hill fort with spectacular views across the countryside. There are many stories about the ghosts that haunt Dunamase – perhaps they are still searching for buried treasure. It is said the treasure lies beneath the castle, but is guarded by a hell hound with flaming eyes.

Castle Roche Castle was built by the de Verdun family around 1236. After her husband's death, Rohesia de Verdun had to try to get the building completed herself. She achieved it by offering her hand in marriage to the man who would complete the castle. A man stepped up and finished the construction and came to claim his prize. Rohesia suggested they look over their fine castle from an upstairs window – and pushed him out to his death! It has since been known as the Murder Window, and the man's ghost is said to haunt the place.

Kildare has a Norman motte-and-bailey castle, but the town is much, much older than that. It is one of the oldest towns in Ireland and was founded by St Brigit in the AD 400s, when she built her monastery there. The story goes that Brigit went to the king of Leinster at Dun Ailinne and asked for some land to build her church. He told her that whatever land the cloak she was wearing covered, she could have. Brigit removed her cloak and spread it on the ground, where it magically grew to cover the whole county of Kildare!

HAUNTED
IRELAND

BALLYGALLY CASTLE

CRUMLIN ROAD GAOL

MALAHIDE CASTLE

HILL OF TARA

CASTLE LESLIE

ROSS CASTLE

FORE ABBEY

ST BRIGID'S STONE

CHARLEVILLE CASTLE

RATHCROGHAN

HY-BRASIL

HAUNTED IRELAND

Sorrowful wailing, bloodthirsty revenge, lost loves, enchanted islands, fallen soldiers, false burials, the murdered and the betrayed – Ireland is said to be haunted by every type of spirit you can imagine. Alongside the everyday world, there is the Otherworld, belonging to beings of a different nature, who sometimes cross over into our world. These are spine-chilling tales of haunted happenings and ghostly goings-on.

Do you believe in ghosts? If the stories are true, Ireland is horribly haunted. Since early times, some have believed in an Otherworld that exists alongside this one. Long ago, the Otherworld was the realm of the Tuatha Dé Danann, godly beings with superhuman powers, who could use those powers for good – or bad. There were said to be portals to the Otherworld in the passage tombs that dotted the landscape. The rumour was that these portals opened on the night of Samhain (sau-in; Halloween), the night when the spirits of the Otherworld could cross over into the human world and cause mischief.

Irish people all know of the sidhe (fairy people or little people), the bean sí (banshee), the cailleach (witch) and the diabhal (devil), and you'll meet many people with a bloodcurdling story to tell about the time they met one of these supernatural beings.

And then there are the people who have lived and died in a particular place and for some reason – usually a very unhappy reason – have not, it is said, been able to rest in peace. They continue to roam, searching for a lost love, or justice, or the answer to the question that won't let them rest.

What do you think? Is it all nonsense? Read on and decide...

Sidhe or sí – both pronounced 'shee'. Sí is modern Irish, but both words refer to the fairies. You might also see the words aos sidhe or aos sí (both: 'ees shee'), which mean 'the people of the mounds', referring to the belief that the sidhe lived in the burial mounds.

Bean sí – 'bann she'

Diabhal – 'dee-al' in Munster, 'dow-al' in Connacht, 'jow-el' in Ulster

BAD CESS TO YOU

A SILLY SUPERSTITION?

The Mayo football team were placed under a curse that has dogged their attempts to win the All-Ireland Football Championship ever since. In 1951, the team won the Sam Maguire Cup – the reward for being All-Ireland champions – and returned home in triumph. But as they travelled through Foxford, they passed a funeral and the priest felt they didn't behave in a respectful manner. The priest was furious and put a curse on them: while any member of that team was still alive, Mayo would never win the cup again. Since then, Mayo has reached the final nine times – and lost every single one.

SAMHAIN

In Ireland, Samhain is a night of witchery and trickery when the spirits are abroad and full of mischief. Long ago, it was thought that Samhain was the one night of the year when the portals, or doorways, to the Otherworld were opened, so it was a dangerous time to be out and about. Huge bonfires were lit to protect people from the roving sidhe (fairy people) and gifts of food and drink were left at the portals – such as the ring forts and passage tombs. These gifts were to please the sidhe and ensure they didn't cause harm. In later times, people made turnip lanterns – terrifying faces carved into a hollowed-out turnip, which was then lit from inside with a lump of coal or a candle. These frightening heads were left in windows or on doorsteps to frighten away any evil spirits that might come calling!

CHARLEVILLE CASTLE, COUNTY OFFALY

The grand Charleville Castle, with its towers and turrets, is a very spooky place. Many visitors have described ghostly figures, a strange mist, a chilling coldness in the air and an atmosphere of dread. The castle is said to stand on the site of an old graveyard, where people were buried alive in the Middle Ages to prevent the spread of disease.

In April 1861, Harriet, the eight-year-old daughter of the third Earl of Charleville, fell down the stairwell when sliding on the banister. She broke her neck and died instantly. Her ghost has been seen many times, sometimes laughing, singing or skipping with a rope. Those who stay the night also swear they hear footsteps in the corridors, the cries of a child, and a chiming clock ... when there is no clock. Visitors who are brave enough can descend into the dungeon. This is said to be haunted by an evil spirit, and those who have been down there report feeling terrified. A strange altar was found in the dungeon, decorated with skulls and hidden behind a wall.

SPIKE ISLAND, COUNTY CORK

In Cork Harbour sits Spike Island, and on Spike Island sits Fort Mitchel. From 1847 until 1883 and again from 1985 to 2004, it was used as a prison. The fact that its nickname was 'Ireland's Hell' gives you an idea of just how miserable it was for the inmates. The most dangerous prisoners were chained and dressed in black, including a veil that completely covered the face with just two slits for eye holes. And it wasn't just adults who had to endure the prison – in the children's block, one hundred boys worked out their sentences.

Many, many people died in the prison, so it's not surprising that there are tales of ghosts roaming inside the walls. Visitors have captured strange, ghostly outlines in their photos, and one photo taken in an empty cell shows a disturbing black mist in the room. This echoes the claims made by prisoners in the 1980s, who said they saw a 'black entity' in their cells at night.

LEAP CASTLE, COUNTY OFFALY

Many people consider Leap ('Lep') Castle to be the most haunted castle in Ireland. One of the most disturbing events occurred in what is now known as the Bloody Chapel. A priest was saying Mass in the top-floor chapel when his brother burst in and ran him through with a sword. The Bloody Chapel still has an unsettling atmosphere. That is no doubt partly because there is an oubliette in this room – a hole in the ground leading to an inescapable room beneath with spikes on the floor. The chapel is just a burnt-out shell now, but locals often see lights there at night.

The Red Lady is a terrifying vision that stalks the castle. She is tall and slender, wearing a long red dress and holding a dagger. And there is an apparition called 'the Elemental', which is said to be accompanied by the smell of decomposing flesh.

The ghosts of two little sisters, Emily and Charlotte, are also seen regularly. Emily fell from the battlements when she was just eleven years old. Sometimes the girls' governess is seen standing watch over them as well. But these are just stories, right?

ST KATHERINE'S ABBEY, COUNTY LIMERICK

This medieval abbey's name in Irish is a mouthful: Monasternagalliaghduff, which means 'the abbey of the black witch'. It is named so as the abbess was said to practise witchcraft there.

Once, during a frantic chase, the Count of Desmond hid from his attackers in the abbey, with his wife. While there, the Countess was pierced by an arrow and fell to the ground. The Count quickly buried her and made his escape. Sometime later, a ghostly figure was seen haunting the area and it was decided to investigate by opening her grave. The lady was still there, but her finger bones were worn down to nubs. The poor woman had been trying to claw her way out of her coffin! To this day, local people say they often hear a woman's anguished screams echoing across the valley in the dead of night, calling for her long-dead husband.

The banshee is the **bean sí** in Irish, meaning 'woman of the fairy mounds'. She has a long history in Ireland and is believed to haunt particular families. When you hear her mournful cry in the dead of night, it means the death of a family member is about to occur. No one can escape the banshee's warning. She has often been seen combing her long hair with a silver comb, and some people claim to have come across the comb in the daytime. But woe betide anyone who picks it up! You could be spirited away to the fairy world or bring a death to your own house.

The **battlefield at Aughrim** saw 7,000 men slain. To this day, strange things are seen here, including a ghost dog, sitting and waiting patiently for its master to come back to life.

The hungry grass or **féar gortach** (fair gur-tock) is a strange phenomenon that haunts the land. It dates from the Great Famine (1845–49), when a million Irish people died of starvation and many were buried in mass graves. Some say patches of hungry grass mark these forgotten grave sites. Others say it is a fairy curse. Whatever the cause, the grass looks no different from any other, so you can't tell it's there, but if you step on it, you are overcome with a terrible hunger.

The crypt underneath **St Michan's Church** in Dublin is filled with mummified remains. These bodies were placed inside coffins, but some of these have broken apart as they are hundreds of years old. So when you descend into the underground vaults, you are met with the sight of skeletal remains, skulls and stacks of dusty coffins. The oldest mummy is 800 years old and is called 'the Crusader'. He's almost 2 m (6.5 ft) tall and is believed to have been a soldier in the Crusades. His legs were broken to fit him into the coffin! There is a story that Dubliner Bram Stoker visited the crypt as a boy and it was the inspiration for his most famous book, *Dracula*.

Loftus Hall is a mansion house standing alone on the edge of the Hook Peninsula. It's one of those buildings that looks creepy from the outside, before you even reluctantly step over the threshold. The story goes that one stormy night long ago, a stranger arrived looking for shelter. The family took him in. During a game of cards, the daughter of the house, Anne, dropped a card and bent down to pick it up. When she did so, she saw that the stranger had cloven hooves instead of feet. He burst into flames and disappeared. Anne was never the same again and her family shut her away. When she died, it seems that she never left Loftus Hall. The servants often saw her

roaming the corridors, and locals swear she is there still, which is why they won't go near the hall after dark.

Kilkenny is famous for the witch trial of **Dame Alice Kyteler** and her maid, Petronilla de Midia. Alice married four times, but each of her husbands died young. After the death of the fourth, she was accused of sorcery and witchcraft. She was put on trial in Kilkenny Castle in 1324. Dame Alice managed to escape, but Petronilla was left to face their accusers. Under torture, she confessed and was sentenced to be burned at the stake. On 3 November 1324, she was put to death – the first woman known to have been executed for witchcraft in Ireland. People say that Dame Alice haunts the streets of Kilkenny, but you would think poor Petronilla would have more cause to roam these narrow lanes in search of justice!

Ballygally Castle, County Antrim, is a hotel now, but it's often said that at night there are more ghosts staying than guests! One unfortunate guest sprinted into the lobby late one night in his underwear, terrified by the sound of a child running around his bed and laughing. In fact, there is one room that remains under lock and key and is never used as a bedroom. It's a small room in the turret and it's simply called the 'Ghost Room'. The ghost most often met, it seems, is tragic Lady Isobel Shaw. She gave birth to a son, only to have the baby taken from her by her husband, who then locked her into a room in the tower. Later, she fell from the window to her death. She continues to walk the castle, crying for her lost baby.

Cursing stones were smooth stones that sat in a 'bullaun stone' – a stone with one or more hollows carved into the surface. In the past, people placed a curse on someone by going to the bullaun stone in the morning and turning the stones in the hollows anticlockwise while speaking their curse and the name of the person they wanted to afflict. There are well-known cursing stones at Feaghna, County Kerry, and at Inishmurray.

The President of Ireland lives in **Áras an Uachtaráin** in Phoenix Park, Dublin, and it seems shares the home with some uninvited guests. Surprisingly, one of these ghostly guests is a young Winston Churchill, former prime minister of Britain. There have been sightings of a young boy running wild about the house. This is thought to be Winston as a boy. He lived in the house for a time when his grandfather was Lord Lieutenant of Ireland, and it seems he's reluctant to leave!

MAGICAL
IRELAND

Renvyle

Killary Harbour

Ballyallaban ring fort

Aileen's
Wave

Killone Abbey

Knockainey
fairy rag tree

Comeragh Mountains magic road

Valentia Island

Lough Derg
Purgatory

Knocknarea
mountain

Benbulben

Croagh
Patrick

Rathcroghan
Cave

Slieve Gullion
Forest Park

Hill of Ward

Hill of Tara

Lia Fáil

St Peter's
Catholic
Church

Christ Church
Cathedral

St Brigid's Well

MAGICAL IRELAND

From the earliest times, Ireland has been a place of magic and magical tales. The oldest and most powerful magic is that of the sidhe, the fairies or little people. They live in the Otherworld, but they can cross over into the human world and can carry humans back to their realm as well. Irish people have traditionally believed that the supernatural world exists right alongside our normal world. This is why fairy trees are respected and why the festivals of seasons are still observed. There is magic all around, and you must be careful not to get on its bad side!

A liminal place is a place that exists between two worlds and provides a gateway between them. There are two famous such places: Oweynagat in County Roscommon and St Patrick's Purgatory in County Donegal. Rathcroghan (Cruachan Aí) was a royal site for 2,000 years. It is here you will find Oweynagat, 'the cave of the cats', which is said to be a portal to the Otherworld and a site of ancient and powerful magic. It would take a brave person to linger here as dark falls on Halloween night! Station Island in Lough Derg is an ancient site of Christian pilgrimage, said to be an entrance to purgatory. This gateway was closed by Papal Order in 1632 and remains firmly shut and locked to this day, to protect those above ground from any dark powers that may exist in the pit of purgatory.

When Christianity arrived in Ireland in the fourth century, magical thinking began to be seen as dangerous thinking. People were encouraged to turn away from such strange ideas. But the old stories are told still – and many heed their warnings.

THE FESTIVALS OF THE SEASONS

There are four major festivals that are celebrated as times when there is both good and bad magic abroad in the land.

The festival of Imbolc (im-bullock) takes place on 1 February and marks the beginning of spring. In the old times, it was associated with the pagan goddess Brigid, while nowadays it is the feast day of Saint Brigid. Food and drink would be set aside for Brigid and a bed made up for her, because it was said she walked among the people on the night of Imbolc and blessed those who were virtuous.

The festival of Bealtaine (beyowl-t'-na) was celebrated on 1 May to mark the joyous return of the sun after the long months of winter. Huge bonfires were lit. The fire and smoke were considered to hold good magic that would protect the people and their livestock for the year to come. This was why people walked their cattle around the fires and sometimes leaped over the flames or embers themselves. They also ritually put out the fires in their hearths at home – something they never did at any other time. But on Bealtaine, the fire in people's homes was quenched and then relit from the sacred bonfire.

Traditionally, the festival of Lughnasa (lew-nasa) was marked on 1 August. It is the festival of the harvest, when the time comes to gather in the crops and prepare for winter. It was named after the god Lugh and sacrifices were made to him, to ensure the harvest would be bountiful.

Finally, the festival of Samhain (sau-in) was celebrated on 1 November. On all festival nights, this world and the Otherworld drew closer and magic could occur, but on the night of Samhain the portals between the two worlds were thought to swing wide. The inhabitants of the Otherworld could wander at will, causing mischief ... or worse.

FAIRY CHANGELINGS

Stories of changeling children are told throughout Europe. In Ireland, it is said that a beautiful human child provokes the envy of the fairy folk. In the dead of night, while the devoted parents are sleeping, the sidhe creep through a window and steal away the human child, leaving a changeling in its place. This changeling can be a fairy baby or an elderly fairy who is nearing death – the sidhe want them to live a life of comfort, being swaddled and cared for. A magical spell is cast to trick the parents into believing they are looking at their own baby, when in fact there is a sickly, grotesque magical being in their midst. This nightmarish story struck fear into the hearts of parents. They would search their baby for any signs of being a changeling, such as being thin and wizened, being voraciously hungry, or having dark eyes that held a wisdom far beyond the child's years.

BENBULBEN, COUNTY SLIGO

The windswept mountain of Benbulben has long been regarded as a magical and sacred site. With its high sides and level summit, Ireland's table-top mountain is said to be an important place for the fairy people of the Otherworld. Its stony grey heart contains grottos and caverns and dark corridors, as well as the highest cave in Ireland. There are two 'fairy doors' high up on the cliffside, inaccessible to humans, sheep or goats. One is marked by a square patch of white stone. The other is a black patch in a hollow. It is said that these doors swing open at night and troops of fairy folk surge out into our world.

MOG RUITH

One of the most powerful magical figures in Irish history is the druid Mog Ruith, who lived on Valentia Island, off the coast of Kerry. He was fearsomely powerful, able to command the elements of fire, water, air and earth. He rode in a fantastical flying machine that was said to blind any who saw it, deafen any who heard it and kill anyone struck by it. Mog Ruith was blind, but his magic was unequalled. If you were going to do battle, you definitely wanted Mog Ruith and his magic on your side!

AILEEN'S WAVE, COUNTY CLARE

The Cliffs of Moher tower up to 213 m (700 ft) above the wild Atlantic Ocean in County Clare. Standing on the cliffs and looking out over the rolling waves is a thrilling experience. Most people watch from a safe distance, but there are some who hike down the steep cliffs to go out into the raging swell. They do so because of Aileen's Wave. This is one of the biggest waves in the world and it attracts professional surfers who want to conquer it. According to legend, the wave has magical origins. When St Patrick first arrived in Ireland, preaching the Christian religion, the ancient ones of the Tuatha Dé Danann were very angry at this challenge to their ruling magic. In a fury, seven of the gods turned themselves into horses and galloped away to the caves on Kilcornan in the Burren. One day, many years later, seven foals ran out of the cave, took fright at the bright daylight after their years of exile in darkness, and bolted straight over the Cliffs of Moher, plunging into the sea. The spot where they entered the water and disappeared into the Otherworld is known as Aill na Searrach, or Foals' Leap. Their supernatural energy is harnessed by the waves at this point, creating the massive Aileen's Wave when conditions are right. The wave can be up to 15 m (50 ft) high and draws surfers from all over the world.

WOULD YOU BELIEVE IT?

An Bradán Feasa (an bra-dawn fa-sa; The Salmon of Knowledge) is a story that draws on a belief in water wisdom. The poet Finn Eces, who was Fionn MacCumhaill's teacher, spent seven years fishing the River Boyne, determined to catch the legendary salmon of knowledge. This mighty fish held all the world's knowledge and this would pass to the person who ate its flesh. Finally, Finn snared the salmon in his net. He instructed Fionn to cook the fish but not to touch a morsel. Fionn did as he was told, but while cooking the magical salmon, he burned his thumb and stuck it in his mouth. The wisdom of the world passed to Fionn, and poor Finn lost his chance to gain the power of infinite knowledge!

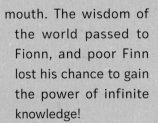

The **wishing stone on Tory Island** has the magic to grant wishes. It is a flat-topped rock jutting out from a cliff. The legend says that if you can manage to throw and land three stones on its flat top, your wish will be granted.

Ireland has a strong tradition of **leprechauns** – magical little creatures of the fairy world. They are said to have buried their pots of gold at the end of the rainbow. They love a bit of mischief, so if you do come across one out walking, you must have your wits about you.

There are many **fairy trees** across Ireland. To this day, people will not harm or fell them for fear of angering the sidhe. This is why you'll often see a tree standing alone in the centre of a field. The farmer works around it, never daring to cut it down. Hawthorn and ash trees are preferred by the sidhe, who dwell in them and bestow magic on them, which is why druids used their branches for their wands.

Rag trees are fairy trees that are festooned with objects and offerings left by people who have wishes they want the fairies to grant. If you see a hawthorn or ash tree decorated with colourful ribbons, coins and beads, each one represents a wish whispered to the fairies. There are two famous rag trees on the Hill of Tara, another at the Athgreany stone circle site in County Wicklow, and a much-visited one at St Brigid's holy well in County Kildare.

Holy wells are often found near fairy trees. They are formed by underground springs that rise up to the surface. The place where they emerge is considered

sacred. They are a very old source of magic, said to bestow wisdom, to heal the sick and to connect this world to the Otherworld.

Knocknarea mountain in County Sligo has an ancient history and feels like a magical place. There are twenty-seven caves puncturing its north side and evidence of human activity dating right back to Mesolithic and Neolithic times. The hidden and very beautiful Glen of Knocknarea certainly has an atmosphere of magic. A narrow track leads into the glen, formed by a huge crack in the mountain's limestone that has created a long and wild valley, where ferns and hazel thickets thrive. It feels like somewhere that spirits and fairies would roam and dance. High up at the top of the mountain is the final resting place of the mighty Queen Méabh, one of Ireland's finest warriors. The spot is marked by a large cairn of stones forming a triangle. It is said that Méabh is buried inside, standing upright and facing her enemies in Ulster.

Ireland has a strange phenomenon of **magic roads**. There are certain places where you can park your car, let off the handbrake, and find the car beginning to move uphill of its own accord! The most famous magic roads are in the Comeragh Mountains, at Benbulben in County Sligo, in the Cooley Mountains in County Louth and in the Dublin/Wicklow mountains. The scientific explanation is that this is an optical illusion – your eyes are deceiving you. The magical explanation is that it's the little people enjoying a spot of mischief at your expense!

The **merrow** are magical sea folk, male and female, who are closely associated with the west coast. They are much like mermaids. It is said that they collect the souls of drowned sailors and keep them in 'soul cages' – wooden boxes like lobster pots – in their underwater homes. A merrow was said to swim regularly into the lake at Killone Abbey in County Clare, where many claimed to have seen her gliding through the water. The male merrow is more elusive, but two fishermen swore they encountered one at Renvyle in County Galway in 1936.

Selkies have seal skins, but they can shed these to take on human form on land – often appearing as a beautiful young woman. When they come ashore, they leave their seal skin by the water until they are ready to slip beneath the waves again. It is said that if you find their skin and hide it, the selkie can never return home.

THE LIVING LANDSCAPE

Tory Island

Devil's
Chimney
Glencar
Waterfall

Clew Bay
Achill Island

Killary
Harbour

Raheen Woods

Brackloon Woods

Lough Nafooey

Shannon
Basin

Torc Waterfall

Ballinskelligs
Reenroe Beach

Reenadinna
Woods

Skellig Michael

Beara
Peninsula

Lough Swilly

Pollnagollum

Crom Castle

Croghan Hill

ckross ey

Giant's Causeway

Mountains of Mourne

Slieve Gullion

Carlingford Lough

Lambay Island

Maynooth College

Bull Island

Powerscourt House and Gardens
Powerscourt Waterfall

THE LIVING LANDSCAPE

The living landscape of Ireland encompasses the whole natural beauty of the country, from flowers and trees to rivers and waterfalls, mountains and valleys, animals, forests, beaches, the very stones under your feet. The geological landscape of Ireland was largely formed by the movements of glaciers, which crept slowly across the land, gouging, scraping, hollowing and depositing. Those long-ago ice sheets eventually melted away, revealing their handiwork in all its glory: the varied and unique landscapes of the island of Ireland.

Ireland is, of course, known for its many hues of green, but there is so much more to the Irish landscape than its vibrant patchwork of fields. The whole landscape is alive with colour and sound and beauty. The Celts believed that all living things were imbued with a spirit or soul, from the smallest river-rounded pebble to the highest mountain peak. This is the living landscape – the life that is breathing, growing and changing all the time.

There are the drumlins (rounded hills formed by glaciers) of Clew Bay, the sea cliffs of the Northern coastline, the Mountains of Mourne, the low-lying plains of the Shannon Basin, wide stretches of peat bog, rolling hills and deep valleys, fast-flowing rivers and meandering streams, long and curving sandy beaches. Part of the reason for these many different landscapes differences is the weather.

The 'sunny south-east' benefits from receiving the most sunshine, which is why heat-loving flowers such as lavender thrive in this part of Ireland.

The midlands are scored by hundreds of lakes, giving those counties a distinctive, watery landscape.

The islands in the seas around Ireland have their own fascinating landscapes, from the rocky crag of Skellig Michael to the spectacular seacliffs on Tory Island, and the special bird and nature reserve on Bull Island in Dublin Bay.

It's thrilling to think that the living world we move through has existed for so long, but is always changing and renewing, and that it will be there long after we are gone.

THE TREES OF IRELAND

If you could hop in a time machine and travel back 8,000 years, you'd find an Ireland covered in native forests. Back then, about eighty per cent of the landscape was tree-filled. Nowadays, only about eleven per cent of the landscape is under forest, thanks largely to the impact of humans and their wish to farm and build. But it is still possible to walk in ancient woodlands – remnants of the original native forests. Woodlands like Reenadinna in County Kerry and Brackloon in County Mayo are magical places with an abundance of native oak, ash, alder, hazel, yew and ferns. They show us what the ancient landscape of Ireland would have looked like.

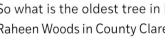

So what is the oldest tree in Ireland? In Raheen Woods in County Clare, the Brian Boru oak tree is said to be 1,000 years old, but this has never been proved. A yew tree at Muckross Abbey in County Kerry also lays claim to being the country's oldest, with a planting date of 1348, making it over 670 years old. In the grounds of Maynooth College in County Kildare is a yew that is believed to be between 700 and 800 years old. But they are both topped by a massive yew at Crom Castle in County Fermanagh, which is thought to be over 800 years old.

As for the tallest tree in the country, that prize goes to a Douglas fir at Powerscourt House and Gardens in County Wicklow. It is a neck-straining 62 m (202 ft) tall!

FLORA AND FAUNA

Wet, squelchy bogs might not sound like fertile places for beautiful plants, but in the summer months the peat bogs are speckled with colour. There's the hazy purple of the heathers, the bright sunburst yellows of bog asphodel and tormentil, and then the soft creamy-white of the bog cotton. The dotted, feathery-white heads of the bog cotton sway in the breeze. If you hold one to your cheek, it's the softest feeling in the world.

Ireland's wildflowers carpet the landscape in glorious colours, especially the reds, purples and oranges of fuchsia and montbretia in the hedgerows and the cheerful blue-purple of a sea of bluebells waving beneath the trees.

Japanese knotweed was brought to Ireland as an ornamental plant, but it has since spread widely, threatening the survival of native species. The same happened with the rhododendron. This beautiful flowering plant was grown in Ireland in the eighteenth century on the lands of the gentry because it provided good cover for game birds, making the hunt more fun. But it wasn't much fun when the rhododendron started to colonize vast tracts of land around the country.

WEATHER

Rainbows are very common in Ireland. When sunlight bends through rain droplets, it produces a rainbow. Ireland gets a lot of rain, but rainbows are one of the many positive side-effects of this.

There are other weather phenomena that make the Irish landscape look even more beautiful. In autumn, the morning mist is particularly striking. It rises from the ground or water and hovers in a bank of white cloud, giving a dreamy, soft quality to the light that looks almost supernatural.

Other weather events are less kind. The sí gaoithe, or 'fairy wind', is a mini whirlwind

that whips up suddenly causing mayhem for the minutes it lasts. Farmers often see this in their hayfields, where most of the field is still but one section of it is being blown around by a violent wind. In the past, the fairy wind struck fear into people's hearts because they believed it meant a fairy troop was passing by.

In recent years, Ireland's weather has become more extreme, thanks to climate change. In 2017, as storm Ophelia raged across the sea and land, a wave almost 18 m (58 ft) high was recorded off the coast of Waterford.

VOLCANOES

Ireland's landscape is marked by a number of extinct volcanoes. The last eruption was about 60 million years ago and its cooling lava formed the basalt columns of the Giant's Causeway. Slieve Gullion in County Armagh was a volcano about 60 million years ago, and Lambay Island in Dublin Bay was formed by an eruption 450 million years ago. Croghan Hill in County Armagh is a favourite spot for hikers. They have a volcanic eruption to thank for the incredible views they enjoy from the summit.

One of the most interesting volcanic landscapes is that at Lough Nafooey in County Galway. As you traverse a steep-sided valley that plunges through the Maumturk and Partry Mountains, you might be surprised to come across a lake with a sandy beach at one end. It looks odd in that place, among the high mountain rocks. This is Lough Nafooey, and it marks the site of an extinct volcano. It's a fine sandy beach and a cold lake now, right there in the mountain pass.

SINKHOLES

Sinkholes can be caused by human error – such as the collapse of an underground mine – or by landscape factors caused by water eroding rock, particularly limestone, beneath the surface. In a moment, the earth gives way and opens a deep pit.

It happened in 2019 on the Beara Peninsula in County Cork, when a large hole suddenly appeared on the side of the road. In that case, a mine shaft had collapsed. A mine was also the cause of a sinkhole that cracked through the earth around a school and sportsground in County Monaghan in 2018. The hole in the ground it opened up was 100 m (330 ft) wide.

A place where natural sinkholes occur is the Burren. This is because it is a karst landscape, formed of sheets of limestone, which is very porous. Here, the sinkholes are called swallow holes and are often the place where a river disappears from the surface, swallowed up by the rock. One such is Pollnagollum – the sinkhole itself is 30 m (100 ft) deep and 30 m (100 ft) wide – big enough for a mature ash tree to have put down roots and grown tall inside it.

WOULD YOU BELIEVE IT?

The **greatest storm** to hit Ireland – so far – happened in January 1839. It was called 'the night of the big wind'. Hundreds of people died and tens of thousands of homes were destroyed.

It's possible to find remnants of the **ancient woodlands** in unusual places. The water levels were lower thousands of years ago, so where there is now beach, there might once have been dense forest. In 2014, Ireland's coast was battered by heavy winter storms, revealing a hidden petrified forest in Kerry. The 4,000-year-old stumps of ancient pine and oak were uncovered at Reen Roe beach.

The **Irish wolfhound** has become a symbol of Ireland, prized since ancient times for its height, power and hunting ability. Wolfhounds were used to protect livestock from wolves. They're not needed for that job any more because wolves are extinct in Ireland. The most famous hound in Irish legend was that killed by Sétanta, who then took on the dog's name – Cú Chulainn – and its job of protecting the household of Culann. Cú Chulainn goes on to become one of the greatest heroes of Irish mythology.

The most abundant bird in Ireland is the **blackbird**. Many people might think that starlings are more numerous, given the incredible murmurations performed by hundreds of thousands of the birds every winter. This is a sight to behold: thousands of starlings, all flying in unison, wheeling and curving and performing aerial manoeuvres in perfect synchronicity. The wings whirr and swish as they swoop and dive, never colliding, never hesitating. The show usually lasts about twenty minutes, then the birds suddenly drop towards their roosts and settle their wings for the night.

Ireland has many **birds of prey**, including the hen harrier, kestrel and buzzard, although their numbers have been declining. Three native species, the red kite, the white-tailed eagle and the golden eagle, became extinct in Ireland. However, in recent years these predators have been reintroduced, which is a welcome addition to Irish skies.

Ireland's smallest resident bird is the **goldcrest**. These gorgeous birds sport a beautiful plumage of red, green, yellow, grey, black and white. Adult birds are only 9 cm (3.5 in) in length. Their nests are constructed using moss, feathers and spiders' webs. The female lays seven to ten eggs, which are tiny – just over 1 cm (less than 0.5 in) across.

One invader of the Irish landscape is the **coypu**. A native of South America

and a member of the rodent family, it can grow up to 1 m (over 3 ft) in length. Some who spot them believe they've just seen the biggest rat ever! The coypu are unwelcome because they are voracious herbivores and can destroy crops and native plants. They also carry some pretty nasty diseases. There have been reported sightings of coypu in Limerick, Tipperary, Galway and Dublin.

Another invader is the **red-bellied jumping spider**, which made its first public appearance in Ireland in January 2020 in a garden in Dublin. These spiders are native to southern Europe, Korea and the USA, and no one is quite sure how they reached damp and rainy Ireland.

There are three **glacial fjords** in Ireland: Lough Swilly, Carlingford Lough and Killary Harbour, which is the best known and arguably the most impressive. It forms a boundary between County Galway and County Mayo. High mountains rise on either side, with the majestic Mweelrea reaching 815 m (almost 2,700 ft) out of the water, forming an incredible backdrop for the deep waters of the fjord. And it is very deep – up to 45 m (150 ft) at its centre, where the black waters drop away beneath the salmon and mussel farms.

The **oldest rock** in Ireland is found at Inishtrahull, off the coast of north

Donegal. It has been dated to 1.7 billion years ago. By comparison, the oldest fossil yet found is 435 million years old – a youngster compared to the rocks that form the island. That fossil was found in Connemara in 2018 and is of a brittlestar starfish.

Ireland has a few truly wonderful examples of **waterfalls**. The highest is Devil's Chimney Waterfall in County Leitrim, where the water falls from a height of 150 m (490 ft). At Powerscourt in County Wicklow, the falls are over 120 m (almost 400 ft) high and fast-flowing. Torc Waterfall in the Ring of Kerry is 24 m (80 ft) and Glencar in County Leitrim is 15 m (50 ft).

Did you know that **moonbows** can occur at night? For a moonbow to be visible, the moon must be full and low, and the night sky must be very dark, with rain broken by clear spells. Donegal is a good spot to go moonbow-hunting, as are the two dark sky reserves of Achill Island in County Mayo and Ballinskelligs in County Kerry.

THE HUMAN LANDSCAPE

EIRE

19

18

H & W

17

BELFAST

16

23

20

21

22

25

24

15

ROYAL CANAL

GRAND CANAL

DUBLIN

14

12

11

1. ACHILL ISLAND
2. HIGH ISLAND
3. CLAPPER BRIDGE
4. SALTHILL DIVING TOWER
5. SPANISH ARCH
6. GALLARUS ORATORY
7. MUCKROSS HOUSE
8. ST. ANNE'S CHURCH
9. BALLYVOURNEY
10. LISMORE CASTLE
11. CURRAGHMORE HOUSE
12. NINETEEN ARCHES BRIDGE
13. BIRR CASTLE
14. TRINITY COLLEGE

15. THE SPIRE
16. GLASNEVIN CEMETERY
17. HARLAND & WOLFF
18. MUSSENDEN TEMPLE
19. DUNLUCE CASTLE
20. MALIN HEAD
21. CONEY ISLAND
22. DUN A RÍ
23. BRÚ NA BÓINNE
24. THE JEALOUS WALL
25. TRIM CASTLE
26. COSTELLO MEMORIAL CHAPEL
27. CÉIDE FIELDS
28. SKELLIG ISLANDS

THE HUMAN LANDSCAPE

Humans have lived in Ireland for at least 12,000 years. That may not be the end – or even the beginning – of the story, as archaeologists are always searching for evidence that will push the timeline back even further. Early humans arrived across the waves from Britain and Europe, seeing a smudge on the horizon that eventually resolved itself into the coastline of Ireland. Since then, people have changed the appearance of the landscape dramatically. Gone are the acres of native forest, making way for farms and houses. We live alongside the natural, living landscape, sometimes protecting it, sometimes damaging it. It is a long and fascinating history.

The built landscape is the work of humans. The structures they erect can be functional, such as forts, homes or stone-lined cooking pits. They can be decorative, like the exquisite shell-studded building created by Catherine, Countess of Tyrone at Curraghmore House, County Waterford. They can also be commemorative, like the many tombs that stand on Ireland's mountains and hills. And, of course, buildings can combine these purposes. Human builders start from the landscape, choosing hollows and valleys for shelter, or hilltops for magnificence, or rivers for food, or hidden places for solitude. The desire to leave a legacy has been important to humans since earliest times.

MOUNT SANDEL, COUNTY DERRY

The earliest human constructions in Ireland are found at Mount Sandel in County Derry and date from the Middle Stone Age. At Lough Boora, in County Offaly, the charcoal remains of the campfires of Stone Age hunters were found, as well as hundreds of stone tools worked by their hands. At Mount Sandel, the finds date to 9,000 years ago and there is evidence of house-building. These early people chose a forest clearing overlooking the River Bann – a good choice for hunting, fishing and shelter. They made holes in the ground and stuck in wooden posts to create a framework, then covered it with hides or thatch. The site contained the burnt bones of wild pigs, hares and birds, as well as salmon, trout and eel, all of which had been cooked in pits. There were also lots of hazelnut shells. The finds at Mount Sandel may represent Ireland's very earliest built landscape.

LIME KILNS

Between the eighteenth and early twentieth century there would have been lots of lime kilns. They were needed to make quicklime, which had a huge range of uses, from white-washing walls to use as a disinfectant. Lime kilns were usually built in to the side of a hill or slope and often looked like a free-standing chimney. A beautiful example at Nobber in County Meath was rebuilt in 2004.

FULACHT FIADH, COUNTY SLIGO

Coney Island in Sligo lies about 2.5 km (1.5 miles) from the mainland and, like Omey Island in Galway, it is accessible at low tide. Once the tide goes out, you can walk or drive across the sand, following the fourteen stout stone pillars that guide the way. On the beach at Coney Island is a small stone structure that fills with water at high tide. For a long time it was known as the 'sailor's grave' because it is long in shape, like a grave. But in 2014 it was excavated and told a very exciting story. The structure is a fulacht fiadh (full-acht fee-ah), or burnt mound, which is a common occurrence throughout Ireland. But finding one on a beach isn't common. It was dated to about 4,000 years ago, right back in the Bronze Age. Fulacht fiadh are thought to be stone-lined cooking pits. So perhaps this Coney Island site was an ingenious way to catch fish and shellfish at high tide, when the water flooded into the pit, and then cook them in the same spot.

POULAPHUCA RESERVOIR, COUNTY WICKLOW

In 1937, the King's River Valley in County Wicklow was a popular beauty spot. It was a beautiful natural landscape, green and flower-filled, and it was home to about seventy families who farmed the land. But in that year the decision was taken to build a huge dam and create a reservoir to cater for the increasing water demands of a growing population. That November, a construction crew moved in and the silence of the valley was punctured by the sounds of building as they erected a 30 m (98 ft) high dam. Three years later, with the dam fully complete, the sluice gate that diverted the waters of the River Liffey away from the valley was closed and the water rushed in, seeping across over 2,000 ha (5,000 acres) of land and drowning the homes of relocated families.

This mammoth operation created the Poulaphuca Reservoir. The building of the dam, and its nearby power station, created the Blessington Lakes, which became part of local folklore. People swore they heard the church bell ringing, and there were accounts of ghostly beings haunting the lake shore. In 2018, the waters receded in a dry spell and revealed abandoned pieces of farm machinery and parts of the drowned houses.

KYLEMORE ABBEY AND GARDENS

Kylemore Abbey stands on the shores of Lough Pollacappul, a beautiful and imposing abbey that was once home to Mitchell Henry and his wife, Margaret. As well as the large abbey, he commissioned the building of a Victorian walled garden in a steep valley about a mile away. Not only did the garden builders have to contend with the V-shaped incline, they also had to coax a garden from bog land.

What they achieved was quite incredible – a garden seen at the time to be on a par with Kew Gardens in London. They transformed a natural bog landscape into a flower-filled garden. Twenty-one glasshouses were built to grow exotic plants, and these were heated by three boilers and 1,500 m (5,000 ft) of underground hot-water pipes.

In 1996, the Benedictine nuns who lived at Kylemore launched a garden restoration project. They employed a garden archaeologist to research the original layout, so that it could be replicated. It took years to excavate the original paths and the work is still ongoing, but the very beautiful walled garden is now thriving again.

CANALS

In the 1800s, the building of canals was seen as an important way to promote a national trading network. The Royal Canal and Grand Canal connected the east of the country with the west. The Grand Canal stretches from Ringsend at the mouth of the River Liffey, in Dublin, 131 km (82 miles) to Shannon Harbour in County Offaly, while the Royal Canal covers 146 km (91 miles) to connect Dublin with County Longford.

ROYAL CANAL

GRAND CANAL

EIRE SIGNS

On some high points of the Irish coastline are huge letters, made of white-washed rocks, spelling 'EIRE', the Irish name for Ireland. These rock markers date back to the Second World War when Ireland was potentially on the flight path of British and German bombers. The signs declared to anyone flying above that they were crossing neutral Ireland – so don't shoot! It is estimated that about eighty-five EIRE markers were constructed. You can still see them in places like Malin Head in County Donegal and Dalkey in County Dublin.

EIRE

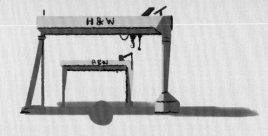

WOULD YOU BELIEVE IT?

Ireland wouldn't be Ireland without its vast network of handmade **dry stone walls**, which serve as field boundaries. The oldest stone walls are those in the Céide Fields in County Mayo, which were built about 5,800 years ago. The method hasn't changed since then – dry stone walls are still built without mortar, each stone selected for its own position. There's an old tradition: you must never touch a stone twice. Once picked up, it must be placed in the wall and not put down again.

If you were to fly over Ireland, you would see **ring forts** – or at least the remains of ring forts. There are ring forts in every county. You will often see their presence reflected in place names – 'fort', 'rath', 'dun' and 'lios' all indicate that there's a ring fort in the area. They were built as community dwelling places, protected by great stone encircling walls. In Donegal, the Grianan of Aileach sits 250 m (820 ft) above sea level. Its 4 m (13 ft) thick walls, built without mortar, are still solidly set in the ground. It is said that the giants of Inishowen lie sleeping beneath the fort, but when the sacred sword is found and removed, they will awake and reclaim their lands.

The **Leacanabuaile** stone fort in County Kerry encircles an area 21 m (70 ft) in diameter. It has a long souterrain – an underground stone-lined tunnel that could have been used for storage or to hide from attackers. Out in the middle of Loughadoon Lake, near the village of Ardara in County Donegal, there is a small island that is just large enough to hold Doon Fort. Standing since the fifth century, it is considered the most picturesque ring-fort site in the country. Its encircling walls are 4.5 m (15 ft) high and over 3 m (11 ft) thick.

The Spire, on O'Connell Street in Dublin city centre, is the tallest built structure in Ireland. It towers over the city street below, reaching a height of 121 m (398 ft).

The cranes of the **Harland & Wolff** shipyard in Belfast stand high over the city. The people of Belfast have names for them: Samson is 106 m (348 ft) tall and Goliath is 96 m (315 ft) tall.

Ireland has a huge number of standing stones, stone circles and tombs of different kinds, so a row of stones on the slopes of Oughtvabeg Mountain, in the Glenelly Valley of the Sperrin Range of County Tyrone, might look like more of the same. But the **Goles Stone Row** is quite special. The eleven upright stones are in a north–south orientation, stretching in a line for 16 m (52 ft). Their

alignment seems to be linked to a small hollow on top of Carnanelly Mountain, which rises to the south. It is also believed that the stones are aligned to the rising of the moon. Whoever erected them 4,000 years ago clearly had a purpose in mind.

In Mayo, near the town of Louisburgh, is the **Bunlahinch Clapper Bridge**. This was built in the mid-nineteenth century, but the builders used a prehistoric form of bridge architecture. It forms a narrow footbridge over Bunleemshough River, is 46 m (150 ft) long and made up of stone pillars and arches.

In Drogheda, County Louth, the viaduct that arches its way across the River Boyne has become a symbol of the town. The **Boyne Viaduct** was completed in 1855 to carry the railway line, which it still does to this day. Trains have been rattling over it for over 160 years, but it's still as sound as the day it was built.

The **Nineteen Arches Bridge** in County Wicklow is famous for being the longest stone arched bridge in the country. It has spanned the Avoca River since being built in 1754–76 and still carries cars and people across safely. The longest pedestrian bridge in Ireland is the Living Bridge in Limerick. It's a whopping 350 m (1,148 ft) long!

Most of the ruins in Ireland are structures that have fallen into ruin over time, but there is one that was built as a ruin. The **Jealous Wall** was constructed around 1760, so that two brothers who had a falling out wouldn't have to suffer the sight of each other! It's at Belvedere House, County Westmeath, and is the largest folly in Ireland. A folly is an ornamental building, usually built for fun by a wealthy landowner. The Jealous Wall might be a folly, but it did serve a purpose – its three-storey, 50 m (164 ft) long façade created a visual barrier between the house of George Rochfort and that of his brother Robert. It's built in the style of a Gothic castle, so that it looks like a romantic ruin of times gone by.

The smallest church in Ireland is also the second smallest church in the world. It is the **Costello Memorial Chapel** in Carrick-on-Shannon, County Leitrim, and it measures a tiny 4.8 x 3.6m (16ft x 12ft). It was commissioned by Edward Costello, in memory of his beloved wife Mary. A carved stone inside the chapel bears an interesting motto: *Ne te quaesiveris extra*, meaning 'Seek not thyself outside thyself'.

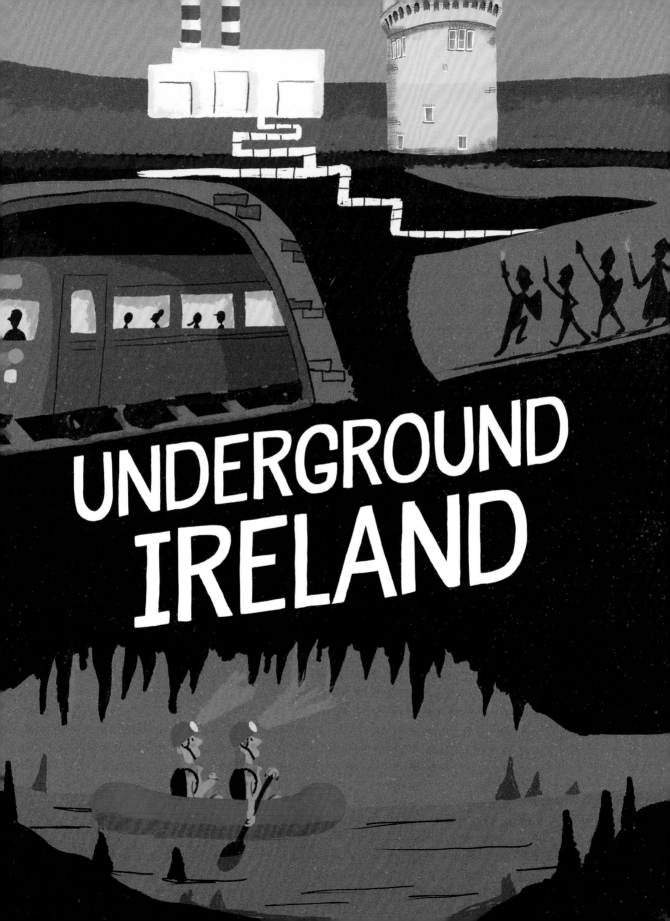

UNDERGROUND IRELAND

Marble Arch Caves

Dooyork

Pol na Leprechau

Arigna

Lough Key Forest Park

Doolin Cave
Aillwee Caves

Burren Geopark

Carrick-on-Suir

Killenaule

Ardagh

Temple Hill Graveyard

Leacanabuaile

Ballinhassig

Releagh

DANGER

UNDERGROUND IRELAND

Caves, mines, tunnels, souterrains, crypts, graveyards, treasure – there is an unseen Ireland beneath our feet. It's fascinating to descend into this subterranean world. The history of underground Ireland stretches from ancient times to the present. In 2003, when the Spire on O'Connell Street in Dublin was completed, a time capsule was buried beneath it, so that future generations can learn about us. The desire to hide and bury often stems from a desire to preserve and protect. In this way, much of Ireland's history has been preserved and protected beneath the ground.

If you could lift off the top layer of Ireland and look underneath, you'd find a whole underground history waiting to be discovered. There is the deep history of the rocks beneath our feet, the caves and the sunken places, the human deposits – like bodies and treasure and archaeological artefacts – and the mind-boggling network of animal burrows and tunnels. One of the most incredible hidden features is the web of mycelium that branches out all across the country. This is the roots of fungi and looks like a mass of white threads. The really amazing thing is that these white threads are the means by which plants and trees share nutrients and information, aiding them in absorbing water and substances such as phosphorus and nitrogen. It's like all the plants and trees 'talk' to each other along these delicate thread lines. Scientists now believe that older trees help saplings to survive and thrive via this mycelium network. It's like an underground internet. Imagine all that's going on right under your feet!

CAVES

In AD928, Vikings attacked Dunmore in County Kilkenny and a battle raged. It is thought that around a thousand people, mainly women and children, took refuge in Dunmore Cave. But the Vikings found them and massacred them in their hiding place. In the 1960s, Dunmore Cave was opened as a show cave with a roof over the entrance and stairs to let people descend into its gaping mouth – and horrible history.

Two of the most visited caves are the Marble Arch caves in County Fermanagh and the Aillwee caves in County Clare. They are show caves, so they are fitted out with lights and steps to make them easy and safe for people to visit.

The most exciting finds at Aillwee were the bones of two brown bears, which have been dated to 10,000 years ago. Jack McGann, a farmer, found the cave in 1944 when his dog chased a rabbit into it.

The Marble Arch caves form part of County Fermanagh's unique UNESCO Geopark region. The caves stretch for an incredible 11.5 km (7 miles) and were formed by three rivers running down from Cuilcagh Mountain and combining underground to form the Claddagh River.

SOUTERRAINS

There are thousands of souterrains across Ireland, so you might well stumble across – but hopefully not in to – one. Counties Limerick, Carlow and Wexford have almost none, while counties like Louth, Antrim, Galway, Cork and Kerry have hundreds. A souterrain is an underground passage or cave that was used for food storage and for refuge in times of danger. It was dug down into the ground and stone-lined, usually capped with stones as well. This meant it stayed dry and free of damp, so it was perfect for storing food. They are most often found in or near ring forts, so it's likely they provided a hiding place or escape route if the neighbours or Vikings came attacking.

BURIED BODIES

The ground beneath our feet contains the bodies of millions of Irish people, their bones slowly returning to the soil. In the Great Famine of the mid-nineteenth century alone, over a million people died. Many of them were buried in mass graves because the sheer scale of death meant that funeral traditions had to be abandoned. Abbeystrowry burial ground in Skibbereen, County Cork, is one such mass grave. Here, about 9,000 local people were buried in pits, all victims of the famine.

In the nineteenth century, Hospital Fields became the nightly haunt of infamous body snatchers. These men earned their livelihood by digging up bodies and delivering them to medical schools to be used in anatomy lessons. Teeth were worth a few coins in those days, too, so they were often removed and kept by the snatcher to be sold separately.

At Mount Jerome cemetery in Harold's Cross, Dublin, there is little pedestal on top of the Gresham Vault. Inside is buried a lady who suffered from taphophobia – the fear of being buried alive or of waking in a coffin. She ordered her vault to be topped with a bell, with a chain running from it to the inside of the vault. She also had a spring lock fitted to her coffin. That way, if she woke up in her burial shroud in the dead darkness of her tomb, she could pop the lock on her coffin, ring the bell and be rescued!

BURIED TREASURE

There is one Mayo man who must surely count as one of the luckiest people alive. In 1998, he won the lottery, becoming a millionaire overnight. In 2001, he and his brother were walking on Geesala beach in County Mayo when they found two 3,000-year-old gold torcs – Celtic neck-rings. The torcs are now in the National Museum of Ireland.

Four workmen digging the Limerick–Ennis railway line in 1854 in Mooghaun, County Clare, discovered the largest hoard of Bronze Age gold objects ever found in Western Europe.

But of around 300 pieces found, only about thirty are still intact. The rest were, it's thought, melted down to make new gold pieces.

The most important find in Irish history is the Ardagh Hoard from County Limerick. Two young men were using a ring fort in Reerasta as a potato patch in 1868 when they found the Ardagh chalice, made of silver, bronze and gold, a copper-alloy cup, and four Tara brooches. The items turned out to be from the Viking age and were priceless artefacts.

TUNNELS

Underground passages are sometimes the easiest way to connect two places. The tunnel at the Guinness Brewery in St James's Gate, Dublin, is a good example of that. When the company expanded in 1873, purchasing more land, it created two sites separated by James's Street. As the public street was in the way, three tunnels were built, for locomotives and for pedestrians. The pedestrian tunnel is still used by staff moving between the two sites.

There can be another motivation for building a tunnel – to hide something or to hide people. In a mark of the times, two nineteenth-century tunnels at Lough

Key Forest Park were built so that the wealthy family that owned the estate at that time wouldn't have to see the 'riff-raff' delivering their goods and carrying out manual work. A similar tunnel was built at the Ards estate in County Kildare in 1852, connecting the grounds to St John's Church of Ireland.

Dublin has lots of secret tunnels running beneath its streets. It is said that during the Easter Rising of 1916, the Irish rebels, under Michael Collins, used the tunnels to evade escape. Whenever the British soldiers got close, Collins seemed to disappear into thin air. In fact, he often disappeared into the tunnels zigzagging under the streets.

WOULD YOU BELIEVE IT?

Ireland has a large population of **Atlantic puffins** on the west coast. They seek out land when they are ready to breed and raise their adorable pufflings. They use their well-shaped bills to cut into the soil and shovel away the debris with their feet. Their burrows are up to 1 m (2–3 ft) long and lined with soft feathers and grass to keep their one egg per year warm and cosy.

A **badger sett** in Dunleer, County Louth, was investigated by the Department of Agriculture and found to be 1.6 km (1 mile) long and about 100 years old.

Phoenix Park holds the **largest Viking burial site** outside Scandinavia. There are about forty graves, which contain grave goods, such as swords and jewellery, as well as human remains.

Temple Hill Graveyard in Cork had a rather unusual first burial. In 1690, after the Siege of Cork, the intestines of Henry Fitzroy, first Duke of Grafton, were buried in Temple Hill. The rest of his body was returned to England for burial.

County Fermanagh lies over an impressive network of caves, including the deepest cave in Ireland. **Reyfad Pot** is 193 m (633 ft) deep – that's a long way from daylight! The exploration of caves is called spelunking and you'd need to be an experienced caver to take on the dark depths of Reyfad Pot. Another region with an impressive cave system is the Burren in County Clare. It's a karst region of limestone, which results in lots of underground features. Here you'll find the longest cave system in Ireland. Pollnagollum and Poulelva together run for about 16 km (9 mile) of underground passageways and caverns.

Doolin Cave, or Poll-an-Ionain, in the Burren contains the longest free-hanging stalactite in Europe. It is called the Great Stalactite, naturally, and it measures 7.3 m (24 ft) in length!

Deposits of gold have recently been identified in Ireland, and the country's first commercial **gold mine**, at Clontibret in County Monaghan, is underway. Four main areas have been earmarked for exploration: Clontibret, Clay lake in County Armagh, Glenish in County Monaghan, and Slieve Glah in County Cavan. The prospectors believe that Ireland's bedrock could contain one of the biggest undeveloped gold seams in the world!

One of the most important gold hoards discovered was unearthed – literally! – in 1896. Two men were ploughing a

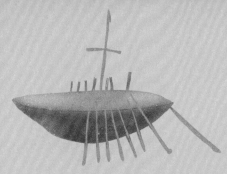

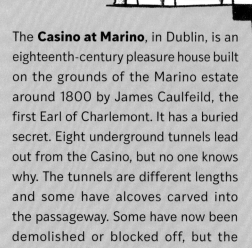

field along the shores of Lough Foyle, at Limavady, County Derry, when their plough hit something hard that wasn't a rock. It was a bundle of metal objects, all encrusted with soil. The men brought them home and washed them. What they were holding in their hands was some of the finest gold objects ever seen. The **Broighter Hoard** is famous for the Broighter boat, in particular. It is the earliest depiction of a sailing vessel ever found in Ireland. It's small and delicate – just 18.4 cm (7.5 in) long by 7.6 cm (3 in) wide. Beautifully crafted, it features benches, rowlocks, oars and a paddle rudder.

Phoenix Park is the largest enclosed public park in any European city. Underneath it lies a rail tunnel, built in 1877. It was part of the direct train service from Dublin to Limerick, to Drogheda and Dundalk, to Galway, to Cork and to Belfast. During the Second World War, it was used to hold emergency food supplies. After the war, it continued to be used to move freight and to shunt trains between the city's two biggest stations – Heuston and Connolly – but it wasn't open to commuter traffic. But in 2016, it was rejuvenated and reopened as a train line from County Kildare into the city centre.

The **Casino at Marino**, in Dublin, is an eighteenth-century pleasure house built on the grounds of the Marino estate around 1800 by James Caulfeild, the first Earl of Charlemont. It has a buried secret. Eight underground tunnels lead out from the Casino, but no one knows why. The tunnels are different lengths and some have alcoves carved into the passageway. Some have now been demolished or blocked off, but the mystery as to their purpose remains.

Dublin Castle's tunnels no doubt have many stories to tell. One story that many people would like to shed some light on is the theft of Ireland's **crown jewels**. On 6 July 1907, the castle was being readied for a royal visit by King Edward VII when it was discovered that the crown jewels were missing. The jewels were the star and badge of the Grand Master of the Order of St Patrick and five gold collars. The theft was a shock to the nation, especially when it emerged that it had probably happened before July and no one had even noticed! The case has never been solved and no one knows to this day who carried out the daring robbery. But some believe that the thief or thieves made use of the hidden tunnels under the castle to make their way in, steal the crown jewels and spirit them away into the night – and into the history of great unsolved cases!

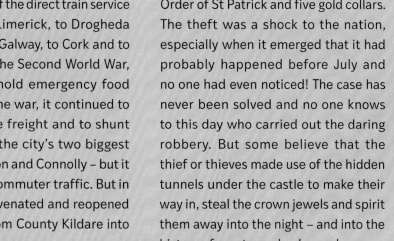

THE
CULTURE OF
IRELAND

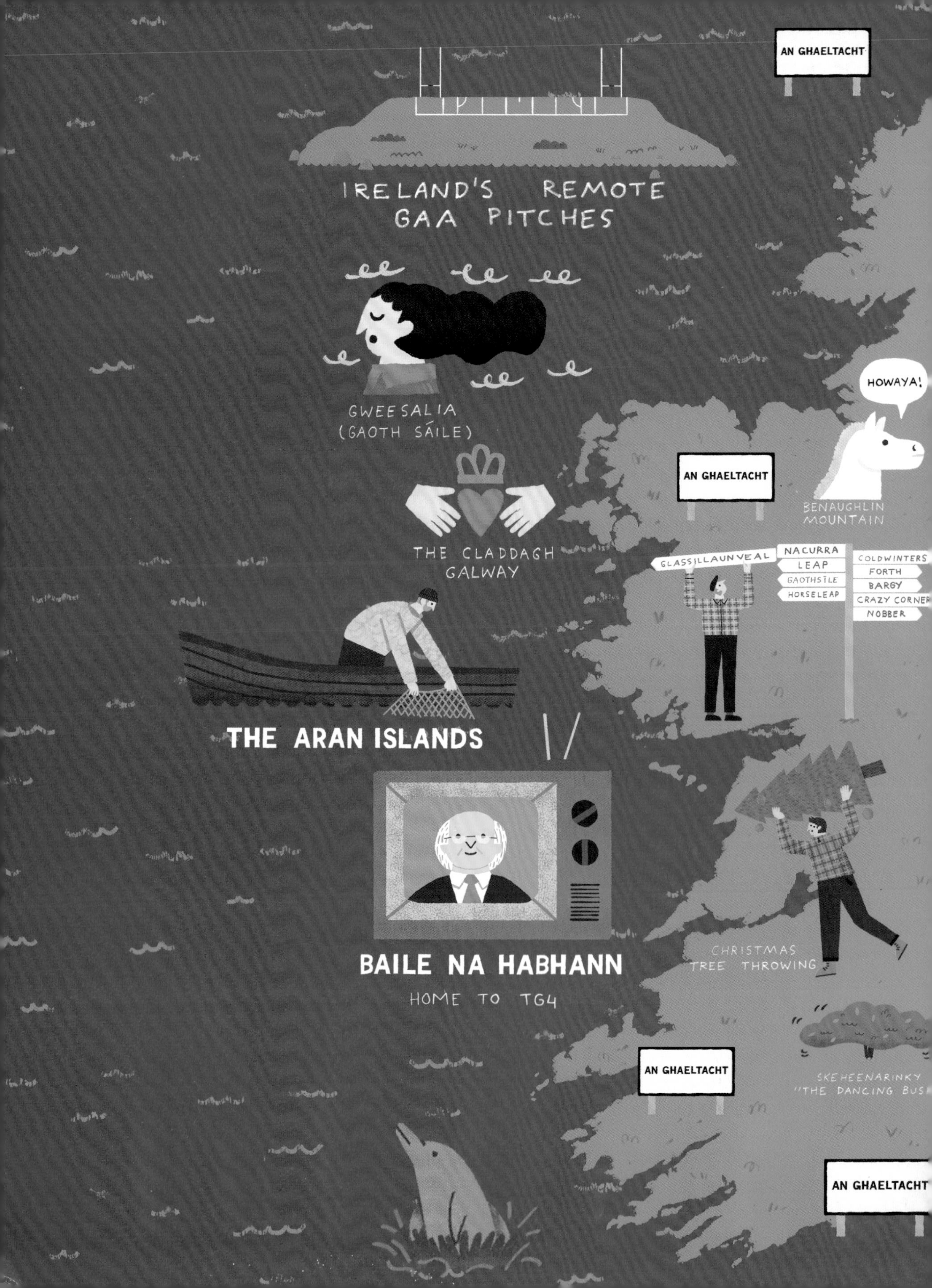

IRELAND'S REMOTE
GAA PITCHES

GWEESALIA
(GAOTH SÁILE)

THE CLADDAGH
GALWAY

HOWAYA!

BENAUGHLIN
MOUNTAIN

AN GHAELTACHT

GLASSILLAUNVEAL

NACURRA
LEAP
GAOTHSÍLE
HORSELEAP

COLDWINTERS
FORTH
BARGY
CRAZY CORNER
NOBBER

THE ARAN ISLANDS

BAILE NA HABHANN
HOME TO TG4

CHRISTMAS
TREE THROWING

AN GHAELTACHT

SKEHEENARINKY
"THE DANCING BUSH"

AN GHAELTACHT

CROKE PARK
HOME OF THE G·A·A
DUBLIN

OG SNORKELLING
CHAMPIONSHIPS

ULSTER FOLK
MUSEUM

GARDEN OF
REMEMBRANCE
DUBLIN

THE RIVER BOYNE
AT NEWGRANGE

AN GHAELTACHT

COLDWINTERS
DUBLIN

FINGAL,
DUBLIN

ST CIARAN'S
HOLY WELL

"BUNDLE OF STICKS"
ROUNDABOUT

DÁIL ÉIREANN
HOUSE OF PARLIAMENT

AVOCA WOOLEN MILL

THURLES
BIRTHPLACE OF THE G·A·A

FORTH,
CO. WEXFORD

BARGY,
CO. WEXFORD

AVIVA STADIUM
DUBLIN

AN GHAELTACHT

LEAP, CO. CORK

THE CULTURE OF IRELAND

All countries have their own culture. It's an important part of what makes a place so interesting to visit. The culture of Ireland grows and changes to accommodate new ideas and generations, but it also has elements that have been present for centuries. The Irish language, instruments, music and dancing are all vital elements of the culture of the country. That's why people love to travel to Ireland and sit in on a music seisiún (sesh-une; session) in a pub or community hall, to watch the dancers' legs twirling to 'The Walls of Ennis', to see the accordion player's fingers dancing across the buttons, and to hear cúpla focail (a few words) being spoken by native speakers. You'll have to come and see for yourself!

What does it mean to be Irish? It means lots of different things to different people, but one common thread is being immersed in the culture of the country. This doesn't necessarily mean speaking the language. Only about 39 per cent of the population can speak Irish. Certainly, the language is important, but it's also about Irish heritage, which means the history and folklore, the music and literature, the sports played and watched, and the sense of humour that is rooted in all these things and connects people. Irish people are known for chat and craic, and it is true that they are a gregarious bunch!

Being Irish really means feeling connected to the place, to the land and to the people, a connection of the heart that travels with you wherever you go and is important to you. Once you're part of the culture, you're Irish.

TRADITION AND SUPERSTITION

Ireland was once known as a strongly Roman Catholic country, but today there are lots of religions represented in the population, and many who choose to follow no religion. However, some of the old religious customs are still followed in many places. The holy well is a long-standing tradition that continues in some counties. There are estimated to be about 3,000 holy wells across the country – plenty are still in use and pilgrims visit them seeking help. It is believed that the waters of the well can cure illnesses. There is very often a sacred tree near the well and this will also be visited during a 'pattern'. On 'pattern day', people walk around the holy well and its site in a particular direction – *deiseal* (day-shal), meaning 'in the direction the sun travels'.

They tie offerings to the tree, such as rags or beads, and pray for a cure for whatever is ailing them.

Another Catholic tradition is climbing The Reek, or Croagh Patrick, in County Mayo. The mountain is 764 m (2,506 ft) high and rises steeply up to its pointed summit. You can still see people doing the walk barefoot, as was the traditional custom, on Reek Sunday, the last Sunday in July.

At the other end of the scale from this good praying is the custom of bad praying – putting curses on people who have wronged you. If anyone ever says, 'Bad cess on you', it means they have put a wish for bad luck on your head.

LANGUAGE

The Irish language is Gaeilge (gay-el-ga), although English is the main language spoken. There are still some places where Irish is the daily language spoken and these are called Gaeltacht (gwale-tocht) areas and are found in counties Donegal, Mayo, Galway, Kerry, Cork, Meath and Waterford. There are also lost languages. In medieval Wexford there was a dialect called Yola that has since been lost. The same happened to Fingallian, the medieval dialect of the area around Fingal in north County Dublin. So you might think the choice now is between speaking Irish or English, but in fact there has been a fascinating change in the language culture over the past twenty years or so. Thanks to freedom and ease of travel, Ireland now hosts seventy-two different languages!

Here are some gorgeously descriptive Irish words with delightful meanings:

bat – sciathán leathair – 'flitter-mouse'

daffodil – lus an chromchinn – 'plant of the drooping head'

jellyfish – smugairle róin – 'seal snot'

PLACE NAMES

In Ireland, place names are given on signposts in both English and Irish. What's interesting is how the Irish name is often simply given an English version rather than being translated into English. This means that if you want the story of a place, you usually need to go back to the original Irish name to find it. The Irish name can be wonderfully informative, as is the case with these places:

Muckanaghederdauhaulia, **County Galway: 'pig-shaped hill between two saltwater lakes'.**

Glassillaunvealnacurra, **County Galway: 'green isle at the weir-mouth'.**

Skeheenaranky, **County Tipperary: 'little thorn bush of the dancing'.**

There are also some downright strange or funny place names, like these ones:

Fiddle Case Pier, Drogheda, County Louth

Bundle of Sticks Roundabout, Naas, County Kildare

Inch Strand, County Kerry, is actually 5 km (3 miles) long!

SPORT

The Gaelic Athletic Association (GAA) was founded in Thurles, County Tipperary, in 1884 to promote the national sports of Gaelic football, hurling, handball and camogie. From this the GAA was born and continues to thrive – it is the largest sporting organisation in Ireland. The All-Ireland Finals are the highlight of the sporting calendar every year and Croke Park in Dublin, where the Finals are held, is now an 82,000-seat modern stadium.

Hurling is the fastest field game in the world – even following the ball as a spectator is hard at times! Gaelic football is quite similar to Australian Rules, and Gaelic players sometimes move over to Australia to play with teams there. In the past ten years, rugby has thrived in Ireland.

Then there's bog snorkelling, where the competitors have to swim through a water-filled trench cut through peat bog as quickly as possible –but you can't actually swim. You wear a snorkel and flippers and you have to flipper your way through the bog. The annual Irish Bog Snorkelling Championships are held in Castleblayney, County Monaghan. Hundreds turn up to compete and dunk themselves in bog mud from head to toe.

MUSIC AND DANCE

The origins of Irish dancing are a long way from the hugely popular *Riverdance* that brought Irish dancing to the world's attention. You have to go right back to druids performing folk dances around sacred trees. Music and dancing were an essential part of ritual celebration, with people dancing at festivals on hilltops, at ring forts, at country crossroads and on the village green.

Irish traditional music, or Trad, is based on the fiddle, harp, bagpipes, accordion, bodhrán (bow-rawn), uilleann pipes and tin whistle. The biggest celebration of Trad is the *Fleadh Cheoil na h'Eireann*, which sees a gathering of around 400,000 people.

The harp (Ireland's national symbol) is the backbone, but the drums are the heartbeat of Trad. The bodhrán started out as a tool for carrying peat and winnowing wheat, until some bright spark had the idea of hitting it with a stick. It was a battle drum, thrumming to the fast beat of the warriors' hearts. The Lambeg drum was also a battle drum and is the largest and loudest folk instrument in the world. The drummers come together at the Clady Day drumming competition in County Armagh every July.

WOULD YOU BELIEVE IT?

The newest sport in Ireland is the skilful and demanding game of ... **Christmas tree tossing**. Yes, indeed! Borrowed from northern Europe, the Christmas tree tossing championships were first held in Ennis, County Clare, in 2012. About 250 people take part, and you can choose your own manner of throwing your tree – like a javelin, or maybe heave it forwards from the waist. Furthest distance wins!

Benaughlin Mountain, on the Cavan/Fermanagh border, translates as 'the peak of the speaking horse'. There are many legends associated with this wild and windswept spot. A long-ago chieftain was said to have been spirited away by the sidhe (fairies) and imprisoned under the mountain. Donn Binn was a famous chieftain because of his beauty and his skill in battle. He was a fine horseman, too. The very best wild horses were said to graze on the upper slopes of Benaughlin, and Donn Binn went hunting

there one day, hoping to catch the finest stallion in the land. He spotted the most powerful horse he had ever laid eyes on – a snow-white stallion. But his fellow hunters could see no horse where he pointed. Donn Binn was bewitched, all part of a fairy spell to lure him to them. He followed the horse for miles, galloping hard, eventually galloping right into a cave on the mountainside. The fairies had their quarry! He lived amongst them for a very long time, but eventually they agreed that he could visit his beautiful land of Fermanagh whenever the clouds hung low over the mountain. On such a night, the great Donn Binn leaps from the cave on the back of his white stallion and races over the land. The horse is known as the Coppal Bawn (from *capall bán*, 'white horse') and at certain times of the year it is granted the power of speech. It was said that the people of Cavan and Fermanagh would gather on the hillside and make offerings. The white horse would emerge and speak with them, foretelling the future. It is also said that they honoured the Coppal Bawn by carving its shape on the limestone of the hillside. Unfortunately, this hill carving – which would be the only one in Ireland – has been lost to memory and no one knows where to look for it.

The **National Ploughing Championships**, known as 'The Ploughing', are held every

HOWAYA!

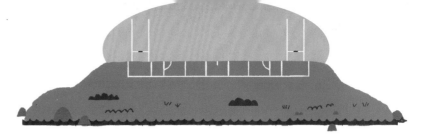

year in September and draw an immense crowd of 250,000 people. They come to watch the competitive ploughing and to celebrate every aspect of farming life and agriculture in Ireland.

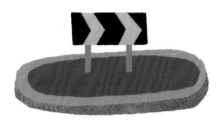

Road bowls is a native Irish sport played on country roads. The game is to use the least amount of throws to shunt your 800 g (28 oz) metal ball the length of a pre-set course along the winding roads. It has a good following in Armagh and Cork, but there are players in other counties too. If you're on back roads around Drogheda or around Cork on a Sunday morning, you might be brought to a halt by a crowd watching with bated breath as a bowler takes to the road.

There are GAA pitches of all shapes and sizes right across the country, but some are vying for the title of **most remote pitch**. The main contenders are Inishturk Island, off County Mayo, which locals claim is the greatest pitch in Ireland! There's a pitch on Inis Oírr in the Aran Islands – the kind of place where you definitely don't want the ball to go long in case it plops into the sea! Carrowmena on North Inishowen in County Donegal and that on Inishmore, County Galway, are also contenders.

Storytelling was always an important artform and pastime in Ireland, right back to the *seanachaí* (shan-a-key; storytellers) and *filí* (fill-ee; poets) of old. The telling of stories was how the people's lives and memories were recorded and passed down. In the medieval period, illuminated books were created, usually by monks. These are handmade books with elaborate and colourful decoration. The most famous is the Book of Kells, which you can see in Trinity College, Dublin. Stories and books remain a hugely important part of Irish culture, in the theatre, in music, in poetry and in all the wonderful authors who continue the tradition of telling the long story of Ireland.

TITANIC

FUN
THINGS TO DO
IN IRELAND

SLIGO

LIMERICK

CORK

FUN THINGS TO DO IN IRELAND

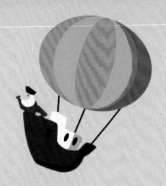

This is just a tiny amount of all there is to see and do in Ireland. It would take a much bigger book to fit in everything! In every county, from north to south and from east to west, there are interesting ruins, prehistoric structures, beautiful views and lots of activities that will get you out and exploring all there is to find out about Ireland. The fun of visiting anywhere in Ireland really is about the people, the places and the stories!

ADVENTURE PLAY

These are places where you can unleash your inner explorer and adventurer – and have great fun!

Tayto Park – theme park and zoo, County Meath

Centre Parcs Longford Forest, County Longford

National Aquatic Centre, County Dublin

Slieve Gullion Forest Park – fairy village, playground, tomb, County Armagh

Fota Wildlife Park, County Cork

Birr Castle and Gardens, County Offaly

Lough Boora Discovery Park, County Offaly

Fort Lucan Adventureland, County Dublin

Lough Key Forest Park, County Roscommon

Castlecomer Discovery Park – Ireland's longest zip wire, County Kilkenny

Croke Park, County Dublin – you can visit the GAA museum, do a tour of the grounds and there's the thrilling Skyline Tour leading to Dublin's highest open viewing platform for unforgettable views across the city.

HISTORY

. . . .

Ireland has a fascinating history – there are so many places to explore it.
Here are just a few:

Bunratty Castle and Folk Park, County Clare

Glengowla Mines, County Galway

St Michan's Church, County Dublin

Christ Church Cathedral, County Dublin

Glendalough Monastic Site, County Wicklow

Kylemore Abbey and Gardens, County Galway

King John's Castle, County Kilkenny

Rock of Cashel, County Tipperary

Waterford Treasures Museum, County Waterford

Foynes Flying Boat Museum, County Limerick

SPECTACULAR SIGHTS

The North Antrim coast is one of the most spectacular stretches of coastline on the island, featuring The Gubbins cliff walk, Carrick-a-rede rope bridge and the impressive ruins of Dunluce Castle.

Croagh Patrick, County Mayo – a holy mountain where barefoot pilgrims undertake a pilgrimage to the summit on Reek Sunday, the last Sunday in July.

Carrauntoohil, County Kerry – the highest mountain on the island of Ireland, if you want a very big view!

The Conor Pass in County Kerry and the Healy Pass, which crosses from Cork to Kerry, are two mountain passes that are renowned for their beautiful views.

Sheeffry Pass, County Mayo – a quiet and stunning road through the Sheeffry Hills, and it comes out at the Doolough Valley, which is one of the most beautiful wild spots in Ireland.

Sceilg Mhichíl, or Skellig Michael – a rocky island off the coast of Kerry, now famous for featuring in Star Wars. It is a UNESCO World Heritage Centre and the beehive huts of its Early Medieval monastic site are still standing.

Howth Hill, County Dublin, has a beautiful cliff walk with wide views of the Irish Sea.

Boheh Stone, County Mayo – this is an extremely important example of Neolithic rock art, featuring cup and ring marks. The stone is an incredible sight in itself, but it's even more incredible if you are there on 18 April or 24 August. On those days, the setting sun viewed from the Boheh Stone appears to roll down the side of Croagh Patrick. The angle of the mountain and of the descent of the sun align to create this extraordinary phenomenon.

Slieve League cliffs, County Donegal – steep and dramatic sea cliffs.

COOL MUSEUMS

W5 Interactive Discovery Centre, Belfast

Titanic Quarter, Belfast

National Museum of Ireland, Dublin – you can see lots of the things you've read about in this book, like the bog bodies, the Ardagh Chalice and the Broighter ship.

National Gallery of Ireland, Dublin – many works of Irish art are housed here.

Science Gallery, Dublin

Natural History Museum, Dublin – known as 'The Dead Zoo' to Dubliners

Giant's Causeway, Antrim County, on the North Antrim Coast.

SPOOKY PLACES

Spike Island in Cork Harbour is now a museum that tells the tale of its 1,300-year history.

Wicklow Gaol has a Virtual Reality tour to really bring the past to life. You can also do the Night Tour – if you dare!

Kilmainham Gaol, in Dublin, is now a fascinating museum that tells the long and harrowing story of the gaol.

Crumlin Road Gaol, Belfast – a tour of all areas of the gaol, including the tunnel that links it to the courthouse opposite.

SHOW CAVES

Aillwee Caves, County Clare

Crag Cave, County Kerry

Doolin Cave, County Clare

Dunmore Cave, County Kilkenny

Marble Arch Caves, County Fermanagh

Mitchelstown Cave, County Tipperary

NATIONAL PARKS AND FOREST PARKS

There are six national parks and twenty forest parks in Ireland. Here's just a selection:

Killarney National Park, County Kerry

Burren National Park, County Clare

Castlewellan Forest Park, County Down

Ballycroy National Park, County Mayo

Glenveagh National Park, County Donegal

Connemara National Park and Diamond Hill, County Galway

Wicklow Mountains National Park, County Wicklow

Florence Court Forest Park, County Fermanagh

Gortin Glen Forest Park, County Tyrone

Tollymore Forest Park, County Down

Portumna Forest Park, County Galway

Glenariff Forest Park, County Antrim

Phoenix Park, County Dublin, which includes the Dublin Zoo

NATURE RESERVES - A SELECTION

North Bull Island, County Dublin

East Coast Nature Reserve, County Wicklow

Kilcoole, County Wicklow

Wexford Wild Fowl Reserve, County Wexford

Capel Island and Knockadoon Head, County Cork

Rogerstown, County Dublin

Bullock Island, County Offaly

Ardnamona Nature Reserve, County Donegal

Murlough Nature Reserve, County Down

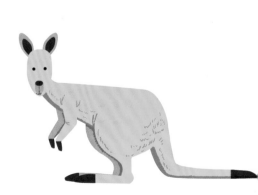

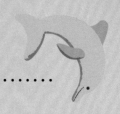

BY THE SEA

National Sea Life Centre, County Wicklow

Dolphin Watching – some popular spots are at: Dingle, County Kerry; Carrigaholt, County Clare; Kilrush, County Clare; and Cork Harbour, County Cork.

Surfing – learn to surf at Lahinch in County Clare, at Carrowniskey, County Mayo and at Strandhill, County Sligo.

Skerries, County Dublin – sea tours out to Lambay Island, where you might catch sight of the wallabies!

Red Bull Cliff Diving World Series – an annual international series of events, one of which takes places in Ireland.

Beaches – among the most beautiful are: Trá Mór, Donegal; Dog's Bay, Connemara; Inchydoney, County Cork; Keem Bay, County Mayo; Tyrella, County Down; Barleycove, County Cork; Lahinch, County Clare; Curracloe, County Wexford.

The Great Lighthouses of Ireland is a list of lighthouses that you can stay in for a truly unique holiday.

Omey Island, County Galway, and Coney Island, County Sligo, are two islands accessible on foot/by car at low tide.

ON YOUR BIKE - OR BY FOOT

Greenways and Trails are paths through some of the most beautiful scenery in Ireland that can be cycled or walked. They include: Wild Atlantic Way, Great Eastern Greenway (Carlingford to Omeath), Great Western Greenway (Achill to Westport via Mulranny and Newport), Waterford Greenway, Limerick Greenway, Grand Canal Way, Royal Canal Way, Boyne Greenway, Avonmore Way, County Wicklow.

EYES TO THE SKY

Armagh planetarium, County Armagh

Dunsink Observatory, County Dublin

Dark Sky Reserve, Ballinskelligs, County Kerry

Dark Sky Park, Ballycroy National Park, County Mayo

ABOUT THE CONTRIBUTORS

THE AUTHOR

Rachel Pierce is a writer and editor who lives in north-east Ireland. She has written two novels for children, *The Lost Bride* and *The Missing Dancer*.

Author's acknowledgements: I would like to thank: Faith O'Grady, Leah James, Philip Parker, Nicola Baxter, Rachel Lawston, Andy Chapman, Dave Macartney, Tayabah Khan, the ten incredible illustrators who have brought these pages to life so beautifully, and Dara Ó Briain for starting it all off so well.

THE ILLUSTRATORS

'The Island of Ireland' – Linda Fahrlin

Linda Fahrlin is an illustrator based on the north-west coast of Ireland. From her studio, she illustrates for clients from all corners of the world, and as you'll see, often inspired by the wondrous Wild Atlantic Ocean.

'Early Ireland' – Diarmuid Ó Catháin

Diarmuid Ó Catháin is an illustrator from Dublin. With over ten years of freelance experience, Diarmuid has worked with a wide range of clients, both Irish and international.

'Warring Ireland' – Alan Dunne

Alan Dunne is an illustrator, author and visual artist. He is passionate about the graphic arts and visual storytelling. His practice reflects his interests in vernacular design and uncovering stories through cultural historical archives.

'Haunted Ireland' – Lydia Hughes

Lydia Hughes is an illustrator and designer based in Westport, County Mayo. She harnesses playful colours and warm textures to deliver simple visual narratives that feel inclusive and friendly yet polished.

'Magical Ireland' – Brian Fitzgerald

Brian Fitzgerald is an illustrator based in Dun Laoghaire. He is the inaugural winner of the Silent Book Contest at the Bologna Children's Book Fair. Brian has collaborated with world-famous 'The Texas Tenors' on their tuneful, Western-style debut picture book.

'The Living Landscape' – Ashling Lindsay

Ashling Lindsay is an artist and writer from Belfast. She has been nominated for the Kate Greenaway Medal, and shortlisted for the Waterstones Children's Book Prize and The Klaus Flugge Prize. In 2020, Ashling won the KPMG Children's Books Ireland Honour Award for Illustration.

'The Human Landscape' – Graham Corcoran

Graham Corcoran is an illustrator and animation designer based in Dublin. He has illustrated two An Post Irish Book Award-nominated children's books, *Dare to Dream* by Sarah Webb and *The Story of Croke Park* by Mícheál Ó Muircheartaigh.

'Underground Ireland' – Jennifer Farley

Jennifer Farley is an author, illustrator and designer from Dublin. Jennifer specializes in illustration for children's books and maps.

'The Culture of Ireland' and cover illustration – Conor Nolan

Conor is an illustrator, printmaker and designer based in Dublin. You can spot Conor's work through its bold shapes and bright, limited colour palettes inspired by the aesthetics of screen printing, risograph printing and collage.

'Fun Things to Do in Ireland' – Donough O'Malley

Donough O'Malley is an illustrator from Monaghan in Ireland, living in Brighton, UK, and working for publishing and advertising clients all around the world.

INDEX